The Films of Adoor Gopalakrishnan

The Films of Adoor Gopalakrishnan

A Cinema of Emancipation

Suranjan Ganguly

ANTHEM PRESS

Anthem Press
An imprint of Wimbledon Publishing Company
www.anthempress.com

This edition first published in UK and USA 2015
by ANTHEM PRESS
75–76 Blackfriars Road, London SE1 8HA, UK
or PO Box 9779, London SW19 7ZG, UK
and
244 Madison Ave #116, New York, NY 10016, USA

Copyright © Suranjan Ganguly 2015

The author asserts the moral right to be identified as the author of this work.

All rights reserved. Without limiting the rights under copyright reserved above,
no part of this publication may be reproduced, stored or introduced into
a retrieval system, or transmitted, in any form or by any means
(electronic, mechanical, photocopying, recording or otherwise),
without the prior written permission of both the copyright
owner and the above publisher of this book.

British Library Cataloguing-in-Publication Data
A catalogue record for this book is available from the British Library.

Library of Congress Cataloging-in-Publication Data
Ganguly, Suranjan, 1958-
The films of Adoor Gopalakrishnan : a cinema of emancipation/Suranjan Ganguly.
pages cm
Includes bibliographical references and index.
Summary: "The first comprehensive study of the feature films of Adoor Gopalakrishnan,
India's most distinguished contemporary filmmaker" – Provided by publisher.
ISBN 978-1-78308-409-8 (hardback : alk. paper) – ISBN 1-78308-409-X (hardback : alk.
paper) – ISBN 978-1-78308-410-4 (pbk. : alk. paper) – ISBN 1-78308-410-3
(pbk. : alk. paper)
1. Gopalakrishnan, Adoor, 1941—Criticism and interpretation. I. Title.
PN1998.3.G66G36 2015
791.4302'33092–dc23
2014049135

ISBN-13: 978 1 78308 409 8 (Hbk)
ISBN-10: 1 78308 409 X (Hbk)

ISBN-13: 978 1 78308 410 4 (Pbk)
ISBN-10: 1 78308 410 3 (Pbk)

Cover image and frontispiece courtesy of Adoor Gopalakrishnan.

This title is also available as an ebook.

For my mother

CONTENTS

List of Figures   ix

Acknowledgments   xi

Introduction   1

1. Things Fall Apart: *Mukhamukham* and the Failure of the Collective   15
2. The Domain of Inertia: *Elippathayam* and the Crisis of Masculinity   31
3. Master and Slave: *Vidheyan* and the Debasement of Power   45
4. The Server and the Served: *Kodiyettam* and the Politics of Consumption   63
5. The Search for Home: *Swayamvaram* and the Struggle with Conscience   79
6. Woman in the Doorway: *Naalu Pennungal* and *Oru Pennum Randaanum*   95
7. Making the Imaginary Real: *Anantaram*, *Mathilukal* and *Nizhalkkuthu*   111
8. The Dream of Emancipation: *Kathapurushan* and the Triumph of the Individual   141

Filmography   155

Notes   157

Bibliography   161

About the Author   163

Index   165

LIST OF FIGURES

Fig. 1. *Mukhamukham*. Sreedharan sleeps. 25
Fig. 2. *Mukhamukham*. Sreedharan on trial in the teashop. 27
Fig. 3. *Elippathayam*. Sreedevi carries the rat trap. 34
Fig. 4. *Elippathayam*. Meenakshi tries to seduce Unni. 36
Fig. 5. *Elippathayam*. Unni snips grey hair. 37
Fig. 6. *Vidheyan*. Patelar dispenses justice. 47
Fig. 7. *Vidheyan*. Thommie awaits his humiliation by Patelar. 49
Fig. 8. *Vidheyan*. Thommie tags along with Patelar. 52
Fig. 9. *Kodiyettam*. Sankarankutty and Sarojini. 64
Fig. 10. *Kodiyettam*. Santhamma ignores Sankarankutty after another escapade. 73
Fig. 11. *Swayamvaram*. Sita mistaken for Kalyani by a policeman. 85
Fig. 12. *Swayamvaram*. Sita after Viswanathan's death. 91
Fig. 13. *Naalu Pennungal*. Chinnu Amma and Nara Pillai. 100
Fig. 14. *Naalu Pennungal*. Kamakshi and her mother in the doorway. 102
Fig. 15. *Oru Pennum Randaanum*. Panki reads on her porch. 108
Fig. 16. *Anantaram*. Nalini and Ajayan on the beach. 119
Fig. 17. *Mathilukal*. Basheer in his cell. 122
Fig. 18. *Nizhalkkuthu*. The drunk Kaliyappan with his wife and son. 133
Fig. 19. *Kathapurushan*. The infant Kunjunni in his mother's arms. 144
Fig. 20. *Kathapurushan*. Kunjunni and Meenakshi as children. 147

All figures courtesy of Adoor Gopalakrishnan.

ACKNOWLEDGMENTS

The seed for this book—I like to think—was sown one winter night in the early 1980s at the Calcutta Ice Skating Rink, an impromptu venue for screenings organized by the city's many film societies, which are now all but defunct. The film, on that occasion, was Adoor Gopalakrishnan's *Elippathayam* (*The Rat Trap*), which had recently won the British Film Institute award.

I remember leaving the building in a daze, muttering to myself, "Perfect! Perfect!"

Shortly thereafter, I moved to the US to pursue my doctoral studies. I did not get to see another Gopalakrishnan film until 1993. By then I had begun teaching film at the University of Colorado at Boulder, where I am currently employed. This time it was *Vidheyan* (*The Servile*), which was shown at the Calcutta Film Festival. It did not affect me as much as *Elippathayam*, but it deepened my resolve to seek out his other films. Three years later—to my very pleasant surprise—I was invited to serve as moderator for a Gopalakrishnan retrospective at the Denver International Film Festival, where he was being honored with the Lifetime Achievement Award. It gave me an opportunity to catch up with the work I had missed and get to know the filmmaker. It also made me want to write about his films.

I want to sincerely thank Adoor Gopalakrishnan for his generous help, encouragement and support at all stages of writing this book.

I would also like to thank Peter Attipetty and Mohan Viswanathan for sharing their vast knowledge of Kerala's social and cultural history with me. Both were kind enough to read and comment on earlier drafts of some of the chapters. I am very grateful to Thomas Palakeel for answering my questions about Malayalam literature and clarifying a number of key issues.

My heartfelt thanks to Ernesto Acevedo-Munoz, Reece Auguiste, David Underwood, Chris Graves, Chris Osborn, Grant Speich and Taylor Mcintosh for assisting me in various ways with the production of this book.

A special thank you to three wonderful friends, Don Yannacito, John Spitzer and Jai Vora, for always being there for me.

My deep gratitude to Sangeeta who, despite her busy life, found time to resolve some of the tough technical problems during the preparation of the manuscript.

I would also like to express my gratitude to the University of Colorado for twice awarding me the GCAH Travel Grant for research in India. It also provided me with GCAH Small Grants for research trips to Washington, DC. I also received an Impart Award to cover some of my travel expenses.

I wish to acknowledge that certain sections of this book appeared previously in *Asian Cinema*, the *Journal of Commonwealth Literature* and the *South Asian Cinema Journal*, as well as in *A Door to Adoor*, which was published in 2006. The chapter on *Kathapurushan* is an expanded version of my essay for the DVD booklet produced by Second Run DVD in 2012.

Finally, as always, I owe a big debt to my city, Calcutta, which has sustained me emotionally, spiritually and creatively all my life. May its epiphanies (on winter and other nights) continue to inspire those who are privileged to call it home.

Boulder, Colorado
October 2014

INTRODUCTION

Adoor Gopalakrishnan, who has been making films outside India's mainstream commercial film industry since 1972, is widely regarded as the country's most distinguished contemporary filmmaker. Despite his fame in India (where he is often described as Satyajit Ray's worthy successor), his films remain virtually unknown to audiences and film scholars in the West, although he has been honored with complete retrospectives at prestigious venues such as the Lincoln Center, the Smithsonian, the Paris Cinematheque and the Munich Film Museum. His 11 full-length features (he has also made over forty documentaries and shorts) have won major awards including the FIPRESCI prize (six times), the British Film Institute award and the UNICEF prize at the Venice Film Festival. France has conferred on him the *Legion d'honneur*. And yet Gopalakrishnan remains one of the most neglected artists in world cinema. Even in his native country, where he has been fêted with virtually every major film award including the coveted Dada Saheb Phalke award and has received India's second highest civilian award, the Padma Vibhusan, there has been no sustained effort to promote his work or even preserve his films.

The critical writing also remains sparse and mostly untranslated in his mother tongue, Malayalam, a language spoken by about thirty million people. Gopalakrishnan's four books on cinema have only recently been undertaken as a translation project. The critical canon in English consists of an uneven collection of essays published in 2006[1] and followed by a standard biography in 2010.[2] The large number of reviews, write-ups and interviews that exist in the popular press tend to revolve for the most part around a fixed set of issues and concerns, the most prominent being that of Gopalakrishnan's status as a humanist. Critics tend to applaud his "broadly humanistic" compassion, his refusal to adopt an ideological position and his avoidance of "the wooly sentimentalism of nostalgia."[3] Others seek to define the "universal truths" that transcend the historical and cultural contexts of his films.[4] This has led to claims that his cinema is both regional and universal.[5] Another tendency has been to read the films as social documents. This, in turn, has generated a fair amount of discussion about Gopalakrishnan's role as the chronicler of the modern history of Kerala, his home state. His cinema, in this respect, is seen as a study of social upheavals and "the rise and fall of political ideologies in rural and urban Kerala."[6] Much has been written in this regard about the centrality of the individual—typically the male individual—as an agent of change and how the films pit such men "heroically against society and state."[7] Thus Gopalakrishnan's persona as filmmaker has been inseparably linked to that of humanist, historian, chronicler and social psychologist.

All but one of Gopalakrishnan's films are set in Kerala, in southern India, where he has lived all his life. Kerala's abrupt displacement from a princely feudal state into twentieth-century modernity is the backdrop for most of Gopalakrishnan's complex narratives about identity, selfhood and otherness. The films deal with eviction and dislocation, the precarious nature of space and the search for home. They are about power and its abuse and the abject conditions of servility it breeds. They focus on guilt and redemption and the possibility of transcendence that lies in choice and action as well as inner transformation. They also allude to the power of human subjectivity to invoke its own state of freedom and thereby transcend its materially circumscribed world. This generates, in turn, a whole other discourse on the role of the imaginary in our public and private lives and its ability to simulate realities that are more real than the real. It results in a philosophical investigation of the nature of reality itself, its perception and its representation.

According to tourist brochures, Kerala is "God's own country," with luxuriant green fields, coconut groves, tea plantations and fisheries. It is also regarded as India's most progressive state, with a 100 percent literacy rate and a highly evolved social and political culture. But Gopalakrishnan's Kerala is a hallucinatory mix of desire and decadence, a place of raw energies let loose, of violent passions and great tenderness, of lost ideals and compulsive power games that often lead to neurosis, madness and death. In every sense, it exists outside all official versions, based on a meticulously observed realism but constructed with the logic of a dream (or nightmare). Poised thus between the boundaries of fact and fiction, it embodies the liminality that is at the heart of Gopalakrishnan's cinema. As Ravi Vasudevan has remarked, "In his films, Gopalakrishnan has transformed the lush countryside, busy towns and animated culture of Kerala into a strange, disassociated place fraught with communicative gaps, menacing inexplicable characters and an overall sense of the impenetrable."[8]

For Gopalakrishnan's generation, which was left disillusioned by the failure of the idealism that was born of momentous events in Kerala's modern history, the need to unmask, to expose the lies and hypocrisies, became a collective wish. The "rewriting" of Kerala became a prerogative. By refusing to endorse the state-sponsored rhetoric of prosperity and abundance, Gopalakrishnan opened up a space in which the repressed could manifest itself. There is thus a fascination with otherness, with lives lived outside established norms and with realities hidden behind the façade of "truth." There is also an attempt to give visibility to those who have been displaced and excluded and describe aspects of Kerala's political (and nonpolitical) life that have been suppressed.

The most potent symbol of otherness is the figure of the outsider. The films document the struggles of men and women who inhabit a liminal space—both real and metaphorical—and deal with conflicts that are sometimes self-generated but more often than not unleashed by larger historical and social forces beyond their control or comprehension. The choices they make—both existential and ideological—propel the narratives forward. Rather than offer us a single, delimiting and predictable stereotype, Gopalakrishnan casts his outsiders in a variety of guises: runaway lovers whose battle for survival brings them to the very edge of society; a stranger without a past who politically radicalizes a community before suddenly dropping out of it; men who perversely inhabit the remains of defunct systems and choose to stagnate; victims of extreme physical and emotional abuse who strive to retain some form of human dignity within their marginalized lives; and women who are trapped within the rigid, restrictive roles prescribed for them by an oppressive patriarchy. There are also those whose otherness and liminality are defined within a more internal space. They include a writer who falls in love with a woman he invents while in jail, cut off from the outside world, and invests so intensely in his creation that it acquires its own compelling logic and sense of life. And there is the schizophrenic who creates and inhabits his alternate reality and produces an elaborate narrative to justify it.

All such Others are integral to Gopalakrishnan's broad-based humanist cinema. He seeks to understand and empathize with their specific social and historical conditions. This, of course, extends not just to the oppressed but also to the oppressors. Every effort is made to place them within the particularities of their lives and within the contexts that shape and define their otherness, especially the liminality that governs their existence. This obsessive attention to historical and cultural specificity in relation to the social and political landscape of Kerala, the framework for these stories, helps his protagonists gain credibility. It also enables us, the viewers, to identify closely with them and understand the problems and issues they face.

Gopalakrishnan has claimed that that even his most apparently political films such as *Mukhamukham* (*Face to Face*, 1984) or those that subscribe to a documentary-like realism (viz. *Kodiyettam* [*The Ascent*, 1977]) are, in essence, studies in human interiority.[9] In fact, his preoccupation with the inner life, with the subtle and complex nuances of thought and emotion, has been consistent throughout his entire oeuvre. He has sought to describe such interiority both from the outside, as it were, through a careful analysis of the externals of human behavior as well as from the inside by inhabiting the minds of his characters. The conflicts in his films—all tangible and real—acquire a whole other dimension as they are filtered through his protagonists' unique sensibilities. Thus the social and the political are not merely external realities but accessed in relation to and via individual subjectivities. The films, in this respect, foreground human consciousness, which becomes a subject in itself in films like *Mathilukal* (*The Walls*, 1989), *Anantaram* (*Monologue*, 1987) and *Nizhalkkuthu* (*Shadow Kill*, 2002) and is crucial in defining the nature of the imaginary in *Mukhamukham*. The understanding that Gopalakrishnan seeks to extend to all his men and women would be impossible otherwise. Even the malevolent villains in his films are humanized to a large extent because we get to know them as thinking, feeling, suffering individuals. We not only empathize with the hard facts of their lives but also with what these facts provoke and become internally. This need to reach out to some of his most unsavory characters, as in *Elippathayam* (*The Rat Trap*, 1981) and *Vidheyan* (*The Servile*, 1993), originates in Gopalakrishnan's vision of emancipation. In fact, it could be argued that all his films are different facets of the search for emancipation in a broken world.

Although Kerala is at the very center of Gopalakrishnan's cinema, the tendency of critics to read the films as nothing more than cinematic documents chronicling historical and social processes ignores the larger ramifications of his work. Gopalakrishnan himself has stated that he's not averse to his films being called social documents as long as their comprehensive worldview is taken into account.[10] Kerala, then, also serves as a foundation for his philosophical inquiries into the human condition that are often existential in nature and universal in scope and revolve around the quest for emancipation. This emphasis on one's conflicted sense of reality and the struggle to transcend it allows us to read Gopalakrishnan's cinema—as I have sought to do in this book—in terms of a trajectory that begins with *Mukhamukham*, a film about the abject failure of an entire community to act politically and ends with *Kathapurushan* (*Man of the Story*, 1995), perhaps Gopalakrishnan's most upbeat and idealistic film about the dissolution of social hierarchies and the triumph of the individual. The films in between, with their diverse scenarios and emphases, seek to define a complex vision of human freedom.

These scenarios often feature guilt, suffering and pain-wracked consciences. Not all protagonists succeed in finding relief or release, but, as in humanist cinema, the attempt—the journey itself—becomes meaningful. More problematic is Gopalakrishnan's insistence that even the most malignant of his protagonists, such as the ex-feudal village chief in *Vidheyan*, are innocent victims, trapped within their ideological inheritance since birth.[11] Their heinous crimes are, in this respect, the deeds of men who have no consciousness of wrongdoing but act out the compulsions that are their legacies. In short, they are inherently good; the real blame should fall on the ideological systems that have shaped them. From our twenty-first century perspective, in a world beset with acts of sheer viciousness and premeditated violence, it is very difficult to condone individual responsibility for evil. In the face of such depravity, Gopalakrishnan's endorsement of goodness and innocence may seem out of touch with contemporary realities.

A more credible scenario in his cinema of emancipation has its source in the body. There are recurrent shots of individuals eating and drinking that are linked to the tropes of gluttony and alcoholism. The men gorge themselves on food in blatant displays of self-indulgence and greed. In *Kodiyettam*, the protagonist's feeding frenzies are the outward symptoms of his wastrel-like existence. He becomes part of a larger critique of masculinity in post-feudal Kerala where males are associated with sloth, apathy, abuse and sometimes a sordid sexuality. With their compulsive physical urges, they are reduced to mindless creatures, consumed by a degrading corporeality. A key question here is whether such bodies can be redeemed. Put differently, can these misguided and flawed men transcend their dysfunctionality and acquire some form of redemptive humanity? In *Kodiyettam* and *Vidheyan*, we see the protagonists evolve from their quotidian states and achieve a tentative self-liberation. They embody Gopalakrishnan's belief in the power of conscience and the awakening of one's repressed moral self to achieve transformation within. Even those who seem stone-hearted and cold experience feelings they have stifled or denied all their lives. Their soul-searching generates a new sense of selfhood and a more complex understanding of the notion of liberty. This vision of human potential and the possibility of transcendence is more realistic than a simplistic faith in innate human goodness.

The Question of Realism

The hyperbolic nature of Gopalakrishnan's realism has earned him, as we have seen, the label of social documentarian. But for him, realism—especially classic realism—is necessary only to establish "authenticity" and "create legitimately what belongs to a situation."[12] Select and essential details serve as the source material, but the goal is to go beyond the surface, to transcend the "objectivity of the image and reach at the very abstract interior."[13] This is achieved not only by restructuring narrative but also by employing resonant and evocative details that arouse intangible feelings, memories and sensations that lie dormant within the depths of the mind. As he puts it, "My aim is to travel with the audience into the epicentre of the dream which arises out of the real."[14] In short, while documenting social living, Gopalakrishnan finds such realism inadequate to represent the multi-faceted, ambivalent nature of reality in both its internal and external manifestations. Thus, he freely incorporates the documentary, poetic, surreal and psychological to create a hybrid form that incorporates and also surpasses mere factual representation. Such an amalgam of styles and forms, singly or in combination, creates a dense framework for the depiction of events. In this respect, his very first film, *Swayamvaram* (*One's Own Choice*, 1972), serves as a virtual proclamation of this concept; his subsequent films endorse it, albeit in less strident terms. However, they rarely go so far as to subvert the very basis of realism. Even the fantasy inserts in films like *Anantaram* and *Mathilukal* are represented realistically and coexist perfectly within the larger realist framework of the films.

Gopalakrishnan's interrogation of realism occasionally draws the cinema into a reflexive discourse on itself. For example, literary texts are frequently read aloud and sometimes take the form of indirect authorial intrusions, disrupting the visual diegesis. Similarly, there are multiple allusions to storytelling as well as the physical act of writing itself, including a whole film—*Mathilukal*—devoted to a writer. Gopalakrishnan wishes to draw our attention to the process that generates texts as well as the constructedness of film as artifice. He also wants us to reflect on the dichotomy of the real and the illusory, which is intrinsic to film.

Some of these ideas can be traced to two indigenous forms of theater that have preoccupied Gopalakrishnan most of his life. One is Kathakali, a highly stylized dance-drama that dates back to the seventeenth century. The other is the two thousand-year-old theater of Kutiyattam.

Gopalakrishnan describes a Kathakali performance thus:

> Kathakali unfolds in a completely mysterious atmosphere, in the dark of the night with hardly any background props—it's the most minimalist theatre you can imagine. Everything unfolds before an oil lamp, which barely lights up the face and hands of the performer. What you see is not real. It is a highly exaggerated presentation.[15]

Perhaps the most obvious influence of Kathakali is felt in Gopalakrishnan's use of chiaroscuro. Characters stand in pitch darkness, minimally lit, or gradually emerge from it into the light and reveal themselves. There are such moments in *Kodiyettam*, *Mukhamukham* and *Elippathayam*. While he rejects the extreme stylization of such theater, its minimalism is reflected in his own pared-down structures where less is often more. Gopalakrishnan has also written about the extraordinary expressive face in Kathakali that can convey interiority with a mere flick of the eyes and that has an obvious relationship to the close-up in film. He is especially drawn to Kathakali's rejection of realism, its emphasis on artifice and the immersion of the spectators in the imaginary, which enables them to reconstruct the play with their minds. For Gopalakrishnan, the whole point is to get to the essence, as exemplified by the stripped-down full spaces of such theater.

In Kutiyattam, a single play can take months to perform (the first act alone can take fifteen days). This sense of duration, stretching almost indefinitely into the future, opens up a complex sense of space and time as well as, "a thousand possible ways of interpretation."[16] Gopalakrishnan's experiments with time in his films could very well be traced to such theater. They include the slow pace of his films where time is often deliberately extended; the sequence shot; compression of time; the coexistence of multiple time levels in a sequence or even a shot; and the audacious use of the direct cut (there are barely any optical transitions in his cinema) through which large blocks of time are erased without any form of transition. These experiments invariably affect the depiction of reality and make the realism of the films more opaque and ambiguous. Also, the sense of unreality they generate within such realism acquires a political function, enforcing the otherness of Kerala outside its popular stereotypical representations.

Kerala and Its Contexts

Kerala became a state within the republic of India in 1956, following the linguistic reorganization of southern India. At the time of Gopalakrishnan's birth in 1941, it was part of the princely state of Travancore and was agrarian and feudal in nature. As a young boy, Gopalakrishnan witnessed ground-breaking political events that transformed this world: the upsurge of nationalism, India's independence in 1947, the assassination of Gandhi (which affected him profoundly), the decline of feudalism and the matrilineal culture of his state, and the birth of the new Kerala within the Nehruvian democracy.

In 1957 the Communist Party won power in Kerala. This was the first time in world history that such a government came into existence through parliamentary elections. It introduced several key legislations and restored land to the peasants through the Land Reforms Bill of 1959, but the euphoria was short-lived. Not only were the communists out of office by 1959, but in 1964, the Party split into the Communist Party of India (CPI) and the Communist Party of India Marxist (CPI-M), thus shattering the myth of a united front. Gopalakrishnan vividly describes the mood of abject despair and apathy in the second half of *Mukhamukham*. Drawn to communism himself—he calls it "the most noble philosophy that ever evolved on this earth"[17]—he never joined the Party and was, therefore, "free to have doubts."[18] These doubts—political and existential—are at the core of the film and underlie most of his cinema.

The communists returned to power in 1967, in 1980 and in subsequent years as well, but things were never the same after the 1964 "betrayal." The 1960s, in fact, are generally seen as a period of extreme disillusionment in Kerala, as was the case in most of India with the failure of Nehruvian idealism. The heady years of nation-building and the optimism it bred in the 1950s were things of the past. Jawaharlal Nehru—India's first Prime Minister—had envisioned a progressive, secular, democratic India based on the Soviet socialist and economic model, complete with five-year plans, but by the 1960s, the dream floundered. There was a significant rise in unemployment, inflation and corruption while economic inequalities kept people divided. The old hierarchies based on class and caste remained intact. With the advent of the 1970s, the momentum for political reform stalled and Kerala became a place "of confusion and the loss of faith in teleologies."[19] Steadily building anger finally exploded in the form of the Naxalite movement, an armed uprising by Maoists.

The failure of the dream profoundly affected Gopalakrishnan's generation and explains the interrogative mode of their films, which attempt to strip away the illusions that underlay the euphoria of the '50s. His own work seeks to define the other Kerala in a series of narratives featuring the tropes of displacement, rupture and dispossession. In fact, the early films portray Kerala in the throes of a severe identity crisis brought on by its sudden encounter with modernity after India's independence and the upsurge of communism. As Ashish Rajadhyaksha observes with regard to *Elippathayam*, Kerala found itself suddenly catapulted from "a regressive, authoritarian feudal state into one ruled by a communist agenda."[20] The enormity of this transition left confusion and bewilderment in its wake. Kerala's emergence into modernity was "a process that it had no means to comprehend."[21] This tragic "history of incomprehension," with its diverse manifestations and "symptoms," is at the core of the Gopalakrishnan's major work.

Such incomprehension is probably most evident in *Elippathayam* and *Vidheyan*, in which the ex-feudals refuse to integrate into the processes of history that are transforming their world. In *Mukhamukham*, we see an entire community reluctant to embrace the moment of political transformation that could liberate them from years of apathy and indirection. Even in films like *Swayamvaram* and *Kodiyettam*, which only obliquely refer to politics, regressive forces threaten to overpower the impulse for change. And the search for self-definition is at the very center of a later film like *Kathapurushan*, which traces the historical shifts within Kerala over a period of 45 years. In almost all these films, an entire community and culture seem to be in a state of suspension, unable to assimilate the new ideas of a reconfigured society. The struggle to open up a space for the modern almost invariably results in a collision of interests, ideologies and ways of living;

the uneasy alliance that is forged is fraught with paradox and contradiction. It is no surprise that these narratives of dislocation frequently refer to home, its abandonment and the attempt to build a new one.

Configuring a New Cinema

Gopalakrishnan was born into a matrilineal joint family within the Nair community. The middle-class, affluent Nairs had an early exposure to Western education under the British and were associated with a certain progressive modernity that would serve Gopalakrishnan well. His family had strong links to the performing arts and were patrons and practitioners of Kathakali for generations. Gopalakrishnan's upbringing within such a milieu also led to his exposure to literature and the dramatic arts in general. In fact, he began to act for the stage from the age of eight and produced over twenty plays, several of which he wrote himself (he is the author of two books on theater) and which were partly inspired by the works of the Malayalam literary renaissance that originated in the 1930s.

For centuries Malayalam literature revolved around *bhakti*, or devotional narratives, until there was a shift in the early twentieth century that "opened up an era of social narratives" and ushered in modernism.[22] The spirit of nationalism in the 1930s helped promote the democratization of modern literature and the strengthening of critical realism. The authors mostly belonged to the Western-educated elite and were called Progressive Writers because of their devotion to socialist realism. The movement began in the 1930s and continued into the 1950s and 1960s when the new Malayalam cinema was taking root. In fact, the New Wave filmmakers would be influenced by the literary modernism that the Progressive Writers had inaugurated; some of these authors would even be directly involved with film projects. Along with their emphasis on realism, the writers sought to "redraft many indigenous art forms and, in the process, re-inscribe them into the narrative of the new Nation."[23] Gopalakrishnan and his contemporaries were drawn to the work of Thakazi Sivasankara Pillai, Vaikom Muhammad Basheer, Kesava Dev, P. C. Kuttikrishnan and others. He would adapt Basheer's *Mathulikal*. His last two films, *Naalu Pennungal* (*Four Women*, 2007) and *Oru Pennum Randaanum* (*A Climate for Crime*, 2008), are based on Pillai's short stories. These films constitute an indirect homage to the movement and its writers.

After graduating from Gandhigram Rural University in Madurai with a degree in political science, Gopalakrishnan worked briefly at a government job, before enrolling in 1962 in the newly established Film Institute of India (now the Film and Television Institute of India) at Pune. His contemporaries included Kumar Shahani and Mani Kaul, who would later become key figures of the Indian New Wave. One of his teachers was Ritwik Ghatak who, along with Satyajit Ray and Mrinal Sen, had laid the foundations of the new cinema in Bengal in the 1950s. Gopalakrishnan never experienced Kaul and Shahani's close rapport with Ghatak and so, unlike them, did not have to worry about overcoming his influence.[24] He learned most from Ghatak when the latter screened his own work and provided shot-by-shot analyses. Ghatak also showed Ray's films and subjected them to the same rigorous analysis.

Gopalakrishnan's first encounter with Ray's cinema had taken place in 1957, when he was a student in Madurai. He saw *Pather Panchali* (*Song of the Little Road*, 1955)—without subtitles—in an open-air theater, and it immediately exemplified for him "radiant truth, poetic and nakedly simple."[25] His lifelong admiration for Ray's work was reciprocated. On a number of occasions, Ray spoke of Gopalakrishnan as being the only contemporary Indian filmmaker of any merit. This led to claims that Gopalakrishnan is the rightful heir to Ray. As the recipient of this accolade, Gopalakrishnan is both pleased and wary, pointing out that Ray liked his work precisely because he did not try to replicate Ray's films and that while Ray can be a valid point of reference, there is "a disadvantage to be in the Ray mould."[26] There are obvious points of convergence between Ray and Gopalakrishnan: a broad-based liberal humanism, universalist in its larger implications; the endorsement of the individual; poetic realism; the aesthetics of understatement; rigorous attention to form; and what Rajadhyaksha has described as "psychology depicted through gesture."[27] But Gopalakrishnan, who belongs to a different and more cynical generation, could never subscribe to the romanticism that underlies much of Ray's early work. According to Ed Halter, "Ray's films glow with a bitter-sweet redemptive humanism. Adoor's films analyze the darker aspects of society and existence with a forthrightness that can afford few comforts."[28] While the quest for redemption is a major theme in Gopalakrishnan's work, it also directs an unflinching gaze at the more sordid aspects of social reality that are largely absent from Ray's work. There is also an engagement with the political in a more direct and emphatic manner than the philosophically detached Ray would ever attempt. Finally, conceptually, Gopalakrishnan's films have a very different spatial and temporal feel to them, drawing not so much on classic Hollywood cinema or Italian neo-realism but on a variety of local and indigenous sources. And his approach to realism, with its blend of diverse, even contradictory elements, differs markedly from Ray's.

While at Pune, Gopalakrishnan was exposed to the classics of European cinema as well as the contemporary work of the French New Wave auteurs. Until then, cinema had been merely a "spectacle" for him, but his time at the institute convinced him that cinema could "transcend entertainment and become art."[29] He became determined "to make good films, to propagate good cinema through film societies, and to publish film literature."[30] Gopalakrishnan had all three goals in sight when he graduated in 1965 and moved back to Kerala. "Good cinema" would come to stand for a cinema grounded in reality, aiming at a truthful exposition of social and political issues within a humanist context. It would shape his filmmaking and that of his friends. And the film society movement would provide the means for creating an awareness of such a cinema.

In 1965 Gopalakrishnan founded the Chitralekha Film Society as well as the Chitralekha Film Cooperative in Trivandrum (now Thiruvananthapuram), which was India's first film cooperative for the production, distribution and exhibition of films made outside the commercial sector. He thus played a pioneering role in the evolution and dissemination of film culture in Kerala that, in turn, created an audience ready to engage with the work he and his contemporaries made. As he points out, with evident pride, "In about ten years' time we had 100 film societies functioning in Kerala. It became a big movement."[31] Soon new graduates from Pune would, like Gopalakrishnan, return to Kerala with dreams of starting work on their projects. The ground was set for a new cinema.

According to Yves Thoraval, since the 1990s, an estimated 90 percent of films produced in India are in regional languages (i.e. languages other than Hindi, which is the lingua franca of Bollywood), one of which is Malayalam.[32] Because Kerala was long in the shadow of neighboring Tamil Nadu's cinema and incapable of producing and distributing its films, only a handful of popular mainstream Malayalam films existed until the 1950s, when the commercial film industry took off. Around the time the first New Wave films appeared in the early 1970s, the industry had grown significantly. Unlike other states that provided monetary support, the government of Kerala remained aloof, so it was left to enterprising producers and cooperatives like Chitralekha to provide financial backing for films that were being made outside mainstream cinema. The Film Finance Corporation (now the National Film Development Corporation of India), which was set up in 1960, offered loans, but they had to be paid back at a high rate of interest. Since the corporation lacked the necessary infrastructure to distribute and exhibit the films it funded, filmmakers were denied a large viewership. After Gopalakrishnan left Chitralekha in 1980, most of his subsequent films were financed by Ravi, an independent producer in Kerala who gave him full creative freedom and support.

Swayamvaram was released in 1972 and quickly became a landmark in the history of the new Malayalam cinema. It was released two years prior to Shyam Benegal's *Ankur (Seedling*, 1974), which launched the New Wave in Bombay (now Mumbai), the heart of India's commercial film world. Around the same time, films by Govindan Aravindan, John Abraham, M. T. Vasudevan Nair, K. C. George and others also made their appearance, sparking off the

New Wave in Kerala. Subsequently, filmmakers from Bengal, Karnataka, Maharashtra, Gujarat and other states would join the movement from their respective home bases and contribute a distinctive regional flavor. Some of them would become nationally and even internationally known while at the same time retaining their identities within their respective regional cinemas. Gopalakrishnan became a supreme example of this phenomenon.

Gopalakrishnan has hailed the emergence of auteur-driven regional cinemas in India as "the most important thing that has happened to Indian cinema since independence."[33] For him, the work of these filmmakers collectively constitutes "a cinema with a purpose—a cinema that was uncompromising in its attitude" which sought "truth" and "did not obey convention" or become subservient "to popular notions of what was good and palatable."[34] Accordingly, he decries the fact that mainstream cinema in India subsequently came to be identified with the commercial films of Mumbai—the "gutter cinema"—while regional auteurist cinema fell under the dubious, exotic label of "art cinema," designed for a coterie rather than a broad audience.[35] His goal has been to reach "the maximum number of people"—the same crowds who generally go to see commercial films.[36] He has, in fact, consistently tried to reach a larger audience by personally supervising the release of his films in Kerala. His aim is to "culture" his viewers but exclusively on *his* terms, "standing not behind the crowd but standing before the crowd."[37]

In writing about Shyam Benegal, who has been called the father of the New Wave primarily because of his Mumbai home base, Sangeeta Datta has defined his work in terms of a Parallel Cinema that exists alongside the mainstream popular cinema (now dubbed Bollywood) and that originated from "the immediate context of political strife and protest" in the late 1960s.[38] She describes it thus:

> Parallel Cinema can be viewed as a modernist project, as an agent of social change with the director firmly entrenched within the premise of nationhood, capturing the contradictions of changing society.[39]

This definition could also apply to the films by Gopalakrishnan and his two most important contemporaries—Govindan Aravindan and John Abraham—despite the fact that their films are very different in most respects. Inextricably bound to Kerala's social and political history, they deal with the larger issues of a post-independent and postcolonial nation grappling with questions of identity and change within the contexts of modernity. Like their regional counterparts, they too were drawn to film as a tool for social analysis and social transformation but adopted different means to accomplish their goals. They had other affinities with filmmakers elsewhere in India: the repudiation of the commercial cinema and its inanities, the rejection of melodramatic theatricality (which had come to dominate mainstream cinema in Kerala), the strong endorsement of a realist aesthetic, a preference for location shooting over the confines of the studio, the use of non-actors, the espousal of humanist values, the inclusion of subaltern subjects and an attempt to reconfigure history and offer an alternative reading. This last issue—the rewriting of Kerala—also made these films narratives of the nation, an allegorical rendering of conflicts, especially those involving modernity and tradition, which extended to the national sphere.

Despite its manifold evolution, Gopalakrishnan's cinema has remained close to the agenda articulated in the '70s by him and his contemporaries within Parallel Cinema. Meanwhile, the rise of Bollywood in a globalized, consumerist India has led to its virtual conflation with Indian cinema in the popular imagination. Not only have terms like *Parallel Cinema* and *New Wave* become redundant, but most alternative forms of filmmaking have been sidelined by the media. Regional filmmakers have found it increasingly difficult to survive and have their voices heard. Along with the problem of visibility, there is also the problem of integrity. The lure of commercial success has, sadly, led to talent being squandered and quality being compromised. In this respect, Gopalakrishnan's cinema is almost unique for continuing to uphold the values and beliefs he has always espoused. Whatever its strengths and weaknesses, it has remained, above all, a cinema of the highest integrity.

Defining a Trajectory

This is the first book-length study of Gopalakrishnan's work, and although I have primarily adopted an auteurist approach, I have chosen not to offer a chronological film-by-film analysis. Instead, I follow the trajectory I described earlier, focusing on the search for emancipation within a Kerala struggling to define itself between regressive forces and the advent of modernity. I cover a large spectrum of issues I have already identified as the staple features of Gopalakrishnan's cinema: the quest for home and identity, the threat of displacement, power and its abuse, otherness, liminality, the role of the outsider, guilt and redemption. Since only *Elippathayam*, *Kathapurushan* and *Nizhalkkuthu* are currently available in a digitized format, I provide a detailed textual exegesis for the benefit of readers who are not familiar with the films and have no way of watching them.[40] As I stated earlier, one of the drawbacks for scholars and students of Gopalakrishnan's cinema is the lack of major secondary sources. While I have taken into account most of the critical positions I defined at the start of this introduction, in the absence of a substantive canon, I have drawn on the filmmaker's statements when appropriate.

My discussion of *Mukhamukham*, probably Gopalakrishnan's most despairing work, is followed by chapters on *Elippathayam* and *Vidheyan*, films about masculinity in crisis in a post-feudal world. Next, I look at *Kodiyettam*, the story of an ineffectual male and his evolution within the contexts of food and consumption. The chapter on *Swayamvaram* describes the travails of a young couple as they grapple with the material and ethical consequences of leaving home and family. I then devote a chapter to Gopalakrishnan's portrayal of women trapped within the narrow confines of their doorways and thresholds in *Naalu Pennungal* and *Oru Pennum Randaanum*. This is followed by a chapter on *Mathilukal*, *Anantaram* and *Nizhalkkuthu* in which emancipation is defined in terms of the imaginary and located within human creativity. The book closes with my section on *Kathapurushan*, which features a symbolic triumph over forces that threaten to retard human progress. If *Mukhamukham* is about failure, then *Kathapurushan* offers the most uplifting vision of human beings under duress and their capacity for transcendence.

Chapter 1

THINGS FALL APART: *MUKHAMUKHAM* AND THE FAILURE OF THE COLLECTIVE

A stranger arrives in the dead of night, transforms himself into a charismatic trade union leader and organizes a strike in the local tile factory; the same man later declines into an ineffectual alcoholic. This—crudely put—is the basic premise of *Mukhamukham* (*Face to Face*, 1984), and the outsider, who is at its center, remains an enigmatic figure, his origins shrouded in mystery. In fact, during the course of the film, he becomes increasingly opaque and unreadable until we even begin to doubt his existence. This sense of unreality is in keeping with Gopalakrishnan's investigation of a community in a state of deep crisis that prefers to invest in the imaginary rather than in the hard facts of their failure. Refusing to acknowledge responsibility for their own actions, they turn to an illusory hope of redemption. By setting the film in Kerala during the politically turbulent '50s and '60s, Gopalakrishnan captures both the euphoria of radicalism as well as the fallout that is inevitable. The crisis he describes is not merely ideological but relates to all levels of a society paralyzed by its own incapacity to live up to its cherished ideals. Even more distressing is the community's inability to forge new values and create a concrete agenda for change. Subsequently, the stranger is expected to sustain their illusions and, in the process, becomes one himself, put on show by a people who have compromised their sense of reality.

The film covers two important periods. The first half ends in 1955, when the Communist Party had made major gains in the state and was poised to win the elections in 1957. The second half is set in 1965, at a time of great disillusionment following the 1964 break-up that led to the formation of the Communist Party of India (CPI) and the Communist Party of India Marxist (CPI-M). The split created a divided society that Gopalakrishnan describes as "spiritually inept and morally confused," with each faction accusing the other of being "revisionist."[1]

Mukhamukham opens with the two-week-old strike that the stranger—Sreedharan—has organized, with both sides refusing to yield ground. The workers hope to stage a complete strike that would shut down the factory and result in a workers' trade union. The source of their inspiration is their extraordinary leader and his total commitment to their cause. One night, an old farmer finds him by the road, badly beaten, and takes him home. Sreedharan moves in with him and his widowed daughter Savithri and later has a son, Sreeni, by her. When the owner of the tile factory is murdered, he becomes a prime suspect and disappears. He does not reappear, even after the victory of 1957.

The film then jumps to 1965, when Sreedharan suddenly returns—once again from nowhere. The demoralized people, rudderless since the split in the Party, have clung to the memory of their hero and now turn to him with great hope, expecting him to lead them again. But this Sreedharan is only a travesty of his former self: silent, withdrawn and mostly drunk. In short, he bears no resemblance to the image they had constructed during his long absence. Because he is increasingly an embarrassment to the community, they have to decide what they should do with him. When Sreedharan is brutally murdered one night, he is immediately deified by both factions of the Party, who bring out a procession to honor their slain leader.

Mukhamukham created a storm of controversy on its release in Kerala in 1984. Gopalakrishnan was branded a renegade who had dared to critique the accomplishments of the communist movement in his home state. There were also endless debates about how the film disparaged communism as an ideology and betrayed the cause of Marxists everywhere in the world. By alluding to the events of 1964, the tragic dissolution of solidarity and the advent of self-serving factionalism, Gopalakrishnan had reopened a festering wound in the Malayali psyche. However, as he has repeatedly said, *Mukhamukham* was intended to be not a political film but a psychological study of a revolutionary who falls from grace, that is, the rise and fall of Sreedharan. Gopalakrishnan's goal was to understand his subject and place him within a framework of interrogation,[2] but most critics preferred to see the film in purely political terms.

While *Mukhamukham* ostensibly deals with a political subject, it refuses to take sides or espouse a specific ideology. It is political in the larger sense of the term as a meditation on issues such as leadership, idealism, otherness, community and, finally, history and time, but these are placed within a narrative replete with ambiguity. In fact, viewing *Mukhamukham* for the first time, it's almost impossible to separate fact from fiction, real from imaginary. Nothing is what it seems. Shirking formula and cliché, Gopalakrishnan refuses to oblige his critics and make a political film with clearly articulated conflicts, ideological positions and a linear, realist narrative trajectory. Instead, *Mukhamukham* functions in a deconstructive mode, undermining expectations and agendas. The concept of the political itself comes under scrutiny and is found to be contradictory and paradoxical. Finally, in the true spirit of deconstruction, the film even negates its own premise as film.

Mukhamukham's unusual and disorienting structure becomes apparent in its twofold division, which metaphorically corresponds to the schism within Sreedharan. Despite certain links, the two halves are quite disparate and collide with one other. They are set apart by a gap of ten years during which we never find out what happened to the man. Such temporal ellipses are common in the film, and they often confuse our sense of past and present. Additionally, Gopalakrishnan uses a complex multiple narrative structure in the first part that introduces several competing subjective voices that try to explain the enigma of Sreedharan. It creates a disruptive collage effect that is enforced through the use of montage. In the second half, there are allusions to sleep, dream and self-projection that further destabilize our perception of the film's reality and that of its protagonist.

By subverting the text through such devices, Gopalakrishnan probes the nature of realism and whether it can, as a representational mode, capture the truth of any given situation. This generates, in turn, a larger epistemological inquiry about knowledge in general and whether it is possible to ever fully know a person—Sreedharan or anyone else for that matter—especially via film. Such questioning of realism leads Gopalakrishnan to address what constitutes fiction and fiction-making as well as the role of the imaginary, all of which apply to how Sreedharan is constructed in *Mukhamukham*. The interrogation of the man, then, both in personal and public contexts and in relation to his success and failure, is at the very heart of the film. But filtered through a ruptured and unstable text, the findings are left open to debate and multiple readings.

Into Memory and Myth

In the first half of the film, Gopalakrishnan's purpose is to define Sreedharan as well as chart his conversion to memory and myth. This notion of transformation is implicit in the long opening sequence in which we see laborers manually transport clay from the banks of a river and dump it onto boats. We then watch how the clay is taken to the factory and transformed into tiles through the collaboration between men and machines in which sheer physical labor is juxtaposed with industrial processes embodied by the spinning wheel and the furnace. Here, in microcosm, is the history of Kerala's industrial revolution, which creates the context for the conflict between labor and capital that is represented by the striking workers. (There is a cut from the fiery red furnace to the red flag of the strikers.) However, more importantly, it provides us with the film's central metaphor of manufacturing a myth or icon, in which men and technology will play a significant role. This idea of construction is invoked repeatedly in the film through allusions that range from basic handwritten forms (handbills and posters) to mechanically reproduced objects such as printed school texts, sacred books, newspapers and photographs and, reflexively, the technological medium of film itself. These disparate forms of production refer directly or indirectly to the formation of the enigmatic Sreedharan.

After this opening sequence, Gopalakrishnan shifts the action to the present, purporting to give us a third person "objective" account of the man and the strike he has organized. In these early scenes, we see the grim-faced Sreedharan squatting with the labor leaders in front of the factory. As time goes by and the strike enters its 65th day, he remains undeterred from his mission. When told that the factory owner is equally stubborn and will not give in to his demands even if the strike continues for a hundred days, his lips curl into a sneer. Soon after, he begins a hunger strike.

At this point, Gopalakrishnan dispels our expectations of the film turning into another socialist realist fable by disrupting the narrative as well as the realism he has been building up.

He cuts abruptly from a series of posters put up by the workers to freeze shots that are sepia-toned photographs of Sreedharan. They show him in fairly banal situations that extend to his public and personal lives—seated in a chair, hanging a portrait of Lenin, walking along a country road, lighting a *beedi*. Only in retrospect do we realize that these images are from the film and thus part of the unfolding narrative. They belong to the future but appear in the guise of the past.

The switch from the moving image to the still image as well as the switch in tense catches us by surprise and undermines our sense of what we had taken for granted as a conventional description of reality. It is the first of several authorial intrusions in which Gopalakrishnan reflexively asserts his presence and makes us reflect on film as an artificial construct and the inadequacies of realism. The intrusion of the sepia stills disorient us further by introducing the theme of death in what has been a living flow of images and events so far. Time is suspended, and what we witness is, in effect, a commemoration through the static images of the man. This is confirmed soon afterward when we see newspaper reports with photographs of Sreedharan. One headline reads, "Homage to Comrade Sreedharan's Memory." Thus the man with whom we had just begun to identify is suddenly declared dead, leaving us lost and confused. We are jolted out of our complacency and our longing to be sutured into the narrative.

The sequence ends with another headline, this time in bold, which asks, "Who is this Sreedharan?" This switches the film to an investigative mode that is dislocating because Gopalakrishnan now thrusts his inquiry onto us. Finding the realist mode to be ineffectual, he invites us to enter the film and participate in the interrogation that becomes, in effect, a tacit admission of his inability to fulfill his role of the omniscient author-narrator. He, like us, must grope his way to the truth of Sreedharan.

Gopalakrishnan begins his investigation by introducing as many as five narratives authored by those who knew Sreedharan well. And he makes us the collective author of the sixth as we try to piece together what is increasingly a jigsaw puzzle. The objectivity of the earlier sequences is now ruptured forever as the film enters a strongly subjective mode. Each narrator faces the camera directly, speaks briefly about the man they knew and then recounts a specific event that is conveyed through a flashback. Their direct gaze at us further destroys all expectations of a transparent realism.

The narrators constitute a diverse social group: Kuttan Pillai, the owner of a teashop that Sreedharan frequented; Sudhakaran, the young protégé, who claims he owes everything to his mentor; Vilasini, a Party worker, who had a crush on the man; the farmer who rescued Sreedharan after his terrible beating. The fifth narrator—who is an outsider, ideologically and otherwise—is the factory owner's henchman. His efforts to woo his opponent were spurned at the very outset.

The first narrative features Kuttan Pillai, who claims Sreedharan was unique in every way, a superhuman creature who survived on tea—especially *his* tea—and four or five bundles of *beedis* a day. He then recalls their first meeting, when Sreedharan suddenly emerged from the darkness of the night and asked if he could sleep in Pillai's shop. It laid the foundation for their long friendship.

Sudhakaran, now in his early twenties, delivers a glowing eulogy about his mentor: "He meant everything to us. He made me what I am." In the flashback of their first encounter, we see Sreedharan hanging a portrait of Lenin on the Party office's wall when the 14-year-old brings him a glass of tea. The sequence is shot with Sreedharan standing on a stool, physically separated from and above the boy as he introduces his future acolyte to "the liberator of the proletariat." In this point-of-view shot, which establishes their spatial relationship, Sudhakaran literally and metaphorically looks up to Sreedharan. The scene is followed by a short one in which we see the boy sitting on the floor reading from a book that Sreedharan has given him. When the boy confesses he has many "doubts to clear," he is told that the mind begins its search from such doubts. Sreedharan's charisma and ability to charm and win converts are in evidence.

After Sudhakaran, it is Vilasini who turns to the camera. As the only female narrator, who was once attracted to Sreedharan, she offers us a radically different perspective by alluding to his extreme shyness with women. On one occasion, he came to visit her brother. Upon discovering that he was away from home, Sreedharan stood outside, too inhibited to be with her alone. When she said as much, he lowered his head, unable to meet her gaze and began to walk away. She believes he chose not to reciprocate her feelings for the sake of his public image, the shyness a mere ruse to mask his desire for her. Vilasini's account transforms Sreedharan into a dissembler who represses his natural inclinations to maintain a clear separation between his private and public selves. The flashback ends with her admonition that women should be part of the male-dominated trade unions. He points out that she is the one who has been asked to organize them. Again, we sense a certain ambivalence here—Sreedharan remains aloof, but his desire to bond with Vilasini is expressed in his sidelong glance at her.

The next person to face the camera is the old farmer who is Savithri's father and who provided Sreedharan with a roof over his head. His remembrance is short and centers on the roles he and his daughter played in rescuing the man from his savage beating. In a flashback, we see the farmer being roused from sleep by Sreedharan's cries and rushing to his side. After the assailants take to their heels, the old man, with Savithri's assistance, brings the victim into his house. Since he knew virtually nothing about his guest or his political activities, he offers us no opinion; his is the only narrative that remains neutral.

Finally, it is the turn of the factory proprietor's henchman who—expectedly—gives the most damaging testimonial, describing Sreedharan as "either a lowdown cheat, or a complete idiot." We see him accost the leader on a country road in order to persuade him to collaborate with his boss. He warns him that the strike is doomed to failure. Some strikers are ready to return to work because their starving families are close to death, thanks to Sreedharan's stubbornness. The best solution to this "hatred and violence" would be to accept his boss's overtures for a private meeting during which—as Sreedharan, with withering sarcasm, predicts—he would be offered a job or a substantial bribe to betray the movement. Since Sreedharan rejects his overtures with open disdain, the henchman promptly calls him a fool. Sreedharan does not even react—he has proven himself to be beyond all temptation.

Cracks in the Facade

From these diverse points of view, a composite image of Sreedharan emerges. The man is physically invincible, politically and morally incorruptible, a charismatic leader who can inspire the young and who puts his political ideals before his personal needs. But it goes without saying that despite their pretense at veracity, each narrator invents Sreedharan, making us question the authenticity of their narratives. Gopalakrishnan compounds the problem by warning us that he has "mixed the real with fiction from the beginning,"[3] which compromises his own position as a reliable narrator. The way the narratives are inserted into the text further problematizes the issue of "truth" because space and time cease to be clear definable units. With the appearance of each narrator, the film switches from third person present to an indeterminate future tense. At the same time, each flashback evokes the past. To complicate matters even more, whenever Gopalakrishnan ends a flashback and returns us to the main narrative, we are unsure whether we are back in the present. Often, it is not even clear whether the flashback is really over or it has simply fused into another. For example, when Vilasini concludes her narrative, Gopalakrishnan does not return us to the present—the events surrounding the strike—but to a previous flashback, part of another narrative, which we encountered a few sequences earlier. He cuts to a medium close-up of the young Sudhakaran staring off screen while Sreedharan speaks to him on the soundtrack. He then cuts to a close-up of a lamp. The abrupt transition throws us off as we are left unsure of our spatial and temporal orientation until we recall the earlier flashback in which Sudhakaran was shown reading from a book while Sreedharan lay on his cot. Can we be sure that this is an extension of that previous sequence, or is it a whole new narrative whose authorship cannot be determined? Much of what is defined as the "present" is similarly opaque because certain events may have their source in memory, thus challenging the "objective" nature of the facts that are being presented.

Most of these facts only confirm what we have learned from the flashbacks; Sreedharan is indeed a dynamic leader, completely and selflessly dedicated to the cause of the workers. He also turns out to be a brilliant orator. We watch him make impassioned speeches in which he repeatedly exhorts his followers to remain united in their fight against injustice. In fact, "unity" is the key word here; he never stops reminding them of the threat from revisionists and turncoats who seek to undermine their vision of a united front. The words seem prophetic in relation to the Party's 1964 split. We also get further proof of the man's extraordinary physical and mental vigor. All through the hunger strike, he does not falter, not even once. He also seems immune to pain, shrugging off a horrific police beating as if it were nothing.

It is via these "objective" facts combined with the subjective renditions that Sreedharan acquires a larger-than-life public persona. What we see, in effect, is an elaborate myth constructed by an entire community that they will uphold during the man's disappearance. The image will become the equivalent of Sreedharan, standing in for him, signaling his presence despite his absence. For his followers, it constitutes the truth, regardless of the fact that it is partly their own invention. They will later invest in this imaginary construct with such ardor that it will become the "real" Sreedharan and, eventually, even more real than his imagined reality. Given this illusory foundation, it makes sense that Gopalakrishnan—reflexively and otherwise—would seek to mix fact and fiction and derail our sense of what seems at first to be the authentic narration of Sreedharan's story. He also begins to chip away at the edifice he has built up.

Quite early in the film, Gopalakrishnan cuts from the striking workers to their starving families. Sreedharan, sitting like a rock outside the factory gates, seems impervious to their suffering. It is thanks to one of his associates—Mathukutty—that funds are collected and the families are fed. Sreedharan, however, remains aloof from this process. Later, the same Mathukutty reminds him that unless the union raises enough money during a complete strike, the survival of the workers and their families will be at stake. Sreedharan's high-minded idealism is under attack for its apparent lack of pragmatics, and the critique extends to his methods in general. However inspiring his presence and rhetoric may be, can he really get things done?

As details about Sreedharan's private life begin to emerge, our skepticism tends to grow. For example, the morally upright leader is found to have a police record. When he has stomach cramps at night, he turns to alcohol (which he has stashed away secretly) to appease the pain. Invited to live with the farmer and his daughter, he promptly makes a pass at her. Twice, we see him surreptitiously burn letters that could be Party circulars or relics from his secret past. These facts all threaten his "clean" public image. But how credible are they? We can never be entirely sure. With Gopalakrishnan having relinquished his omniscient authority, we have to figure out whether the man even exists.

Gopalakrishnan develops these ideas further through his exploration of the image—to emphasize its centrality to his narrative, both as a literal fact and metaphor. When Sreedharan, in the first half, hangs the portrait of Lenin, we see his image reflected in the glass. The two images merge for an instant, one subsumed into the larger iconic presence of the other. Sreedharan's veneration of his political mentor anticipates his own veneration as an image by the people. But as we see him become an image—an image within an image—he also loses all sense of reality for us, refracted endlessly, as it were, through an infinite set of reflections. This diminution of the man into image qua image is unnerving to say the least and a portent of things to come.

Later in the film, when the police raid the trade union's office, the same portrait of Lenin is hurled to the floor and smashed under a pair of boots. As red ink from a broken pot spreads like blood on the shattered glass, we witness the symbolic death of an icon. But just as Lenin would be restored after the communists' return to power in 1957 and his portrait would once again adorn the wall, Sreedharan's photograph would be similarly restored. And it would be this portrait—the bearded face from better days—that would be taken out in the procession following his death. People would turn to this image and regard it, not the alcoholic who returned home after 10 years, as the real Sreedharan. There is thus a fall, a trampling upon, followed by a symbolic resurrection, which applies to both men.

This idea of resurrection vis-à-vis the image acquires complex ironic undertones in a sequence in the second half. The setting, this time, is the building that houses the headquarters of the CPI Party. It has been named after Sreedharan. When the latter pays a visit, he sees his garlanded portrait—the same one from 10 years ago—on the wall. The living man thus confronts the symbol of his commemoration and, by the time the scene is over, it is clear that death and remembrance are ironically the conditions of his staying alive. Also prominent on the wall is the portrait of Lenin we have encountered before. It is in relation to these images that the scene is staged between Sreedharan and the Party chief—Damodaran—his old friend and associate. Both portraits strongly evoke the past, but a past that has no relationship to the present.

Damodaran tells Sreedharan that the Party split due to the betrayal of Marxism-Leninism by revisionist forces from within; the casualty, of course, was the unity championed by the latter. In trying to justify the dissolution of the solidarity his mentor fought so hard for, Damodaran ironically mimics his words. This imitation almost amounts to caricature. It also becomes a pathetic attempt to shift the blame on others instead of admitting to a collective guilt. Damodaran's rivals—the CPI(M) Party members—are engaged in the same finger-pointing as they try to deny their own culpability. As a villager exclaims in disgust, "The air stinks with accusations and counter-accusations between rivals who call themselves communists!"

Damodaran even audaciously insinuates that Sreedharan, by not coming forward in 1964 to define his own position, compromised himself and the Party. He next quotes Lenin about how those who take a stand against the interests of the working class must be treated as reactionaries—implying that the words could very well apply to Sreedharan. The whole scene smacks of the decadence and fakeness that has come to govern political life.

The portraits of Lenin and Sreedharan on the wall confirm this further, since both are now images without substance for a community that once worshipped them as heroes. Ironically, it is only in this form that they are kept alive. For Sreedharan, who has returned from the dead, his only context for living in such a world of shattered ideals is as memory and trace, which his portrait exemplifies. This is evident in the way the camera frames the silent, withdrawn Sreedharan in relation to his image. In short, to be alive, he must die. The present cannot accommodate him on his own terms. If, then, in the first half of *Mukhamukham* we witnessed Sreedharan's construction as myth and image, the second half becomes the setting for the confrontation between man and image.

The Second Coming of Sreedharan

Although this final section begins with reflexive allusions to written texts (school texts and sacred books) and even includes a reference to storytelling (the farmer reads from the *Bhagavatham*, in which a holy bird narrates stories from the life of Vishnu), Gopalakrishnan's style is less elliptical as he situates the action in a new present. He drops the multiple narrative form in favor of a fairly conventional realist unfolding of events. He seems to have reclaimed his role of the author-narrator, and, accordingly, we are less involved as participants in the construction of meaning. But this return to realism is deceptive; he will deconstruct it when the moment is ripe.

In this second half, Sreedharan's radical transformation is evident from the moment he steps into his house. His body sags; he can hardly stand upright or keep his eyes open. And he barely speaks. There are recurring shots of him drunk, or stretched out comatose, often snoring. His withdrawal from public life, coupled with his apathy and silence, make him a complete stranger to the entire community. This is brought out in a marvelous scene in which the people gather around him for the first time since his return, to welcome their old leader. The camera pans over their eager faces, which soon begin to display signs of concern, worry and eventually disappointment. Sreedharan does not show any emotion whatsoever, nor does he exchange any meaningful words with them. The only time he acts and speaks is when he deftly removes a few rupees from an old friend's shirt pocket—money apparently for the liquor den—and tells him that they will not be returned. Before long, he is snoring away (Figure 1). Thus this first face-to-face encounter proves to be an unmitigated disaster. We are taken aback and left to wonder if Sreedharan has finally assumed the repressed self that we glimpsed in the first half.

Later in the film, Damodaran will quote Lenin again: "The proletarian movement passes through various stages of growth. At every stage, a set of people stagger, stop, and drop out of the movement's march forward."

Although the words are not directed at Sreedharan, he becomes their subject as the camera singles him out, sitting in his house, head bowed, silent and unresponsive. Is he indeed a drop-out? Gopalakrishnan has said that there is a revolutionary in every individual, but over time the spirit either dies or becomes dormant. The idea of *Mukhamukham* was born out of a desire "to search for this spirit."[4] Sreedharan is, of course, at the center of this quest.

Fig. 1. *Mukhamukham.* Sreedharan sleeps.

Although what caused the flame to burn out is never completely explained, we see the results of its extinction, which affect the man in every sphere of his life.

Perhaps the most poignant aspect of Sreedharan's transformation is reflected in his relationship with his son, Sreeni. The boy has grown up nourished by stories about his father and the possibility of his homecoming. When he indeed returns, the son expectantly awaits the opportunity to speak to him. As he puts it, "There's so much I want to ask father," but his hopes are dashed as Sreedharan remains in an alcoholic stupor. In fact, they do not exchange a word in the film. When Sreedharan later steals Savithri's money, Sreeni is accused of the theft and receives a thrashing from her. Even when it becomes apparent who the real culprit is, the father offers no apology to his son. The final humiliation for Sreeni is when Sreedharan is found drunk in his school compound; overcome by shame, the son watches from behind a tree.

Sreedharan's relationship with his surrogate son, Sudhakaran, who is now an adult, is framed within the political crisis brought on by the split in the Party. In the aftermath of the break-up, we see Sreedharan's protégé express his sense of outrage at the current situation: "It's all rotten—stinking. There's no relationship between what they preach and what they practice. I just cannot accept it." The bitterness in his voice does not provoke any reaction from his old teacher, who remains silent (Sudhakaran even asks him why he is so silent). Once again, Sreedharan turns away from those who crave some form of contact and communication with him. However, unlike Sreeni, Sudhakaran manages to break through. It happens right after his unjust expulsion from the Party, when he turns once again to Sreedharan, this time as an angry young rebel who promises to "tear the masks off the enemies of the people." He speaks of a small group of determined young men who are willing to face every challenge and put up a fight. The mute Sreedharan's eyes light up, and a faint smile of approval hovers on his lips. It is virtually the only time he is able to transcend his apathy and display something of his old self. But the moment passes quickly, and we are left with the larger question of his silence. Why *is* he silent?

On one level, Sreedharan's silence seems to be the most potent response to the collapse of everything he once envisioned. Faced with the destruction of his cherished dream of solidarity and the idealism that sustained it, he does not have anything more to say or do and turns to alcohol to drown his own sense of failure and the betrayal of his cause. His silence is almost a complete reversal of the one we encountered earlier in the film, when it "spoke" of his inner strength, perseverance and fortitude. It is also the complete antithesis of his eloquence as a superlative public speaker who could move crowds with the power of his rhetoric. It is as if the great orator has suddenly lost faith in language itself and its capacity to bring about change. Such a completely disorienting (and deafening) silence reeks of defeat, withdrawal, helplessness and even contempt for himself and for those around him; it complements his almost compulsive urge to find solace in drink and sleep.

The film also shows how Sreedharan's silence can serve other functions. Mathukutty—who has fattened himself via various corrupt practices—speaks warmly of the factory owner's son. He even proposes that Sreedharan now work for the factory as a cashier—the union will make sure he illegally gets the job over other applicants. He can also count, he adds, on the proprietor's support. To this offer to sell out to the "enemy," Sreedharan does not react with words but with a wry, mocking smile. The combination of silence and mockery constitutes a devastating rejoinder. Later, both Mathaikutty and Damodaran strive to make their former leader endorse their respective parties and thus grant either one a certain legitimacy. Damodaran even gives him a document to sign, but Sreedharan maintains his apathetic distance from both men, refusing to be subtly coerced. His silence thus becomes an effective form of scorn as well as protest at their attempts to exploit and manipulate him.

Courting an Illusion

Along with the failure of solidarity, what is even more tragic for Gopalakrishnan is the inability of the people to unite and act in the aftermath of a crisis. Instead of shaking themselves out of their apathy and responding decisively as a group with a new political agenda, they invest all their hopes in the second coming of Sreedharan. This Sreedharan they covet is the man of the image they have nurtured all these years—the charismatic hero who taught them to combat injustice within a debased system. Having failed to transform his dream into reality, they now desperately want him to come back and fight their battles for them. Gopalakrishnan sees this as an ominous trend that surfaces in the wake of a political debacle. People turn away from reality, from the facts of their failure, to immerse themselves almost wholly in the imaginary. For him, this loss of will points to the larger betrayal of the modern social revolution, built on the premise of unity and collective action.

In his second direct encounter with the people, Sreedharan is cornered by them in Kuttan Pillai's teashop and put on trial (Figure 2). Called "an object of disgust," he is asked to explain what his game is. When he wants to know what he has done wrong, he is accused of letting down the people and their expectations. "It was you who roused them from sleep," he is told, implying that now he is the one who sleeps. Sreedharan typically does not defend himself, but his query is a form of retort to make his interrogators focus on their own responsibility. The scene ends with Sreedharan turning toward Sugathan, the man who has staged the trial. Sugathan cannot look him in

Fig. 2. *Mukhamukham*. Sreedharan on trial in the teashop.

the eye and turns his face away. It is a crucial moment in the film because Sreedharan, who usually keeps his eyes lowered, suddenly asserts his gaze. It results in discomfiture and guilt as Sugathan and his cronies come face to face with the sad and inevitable truth that they have only themselves to blame.

The question at the end of the film is: What should be done with Sreedharan? As a man in a state of disgrace, he is a source of great embarrassment to the community. But it is not merely an issue of the hero not conforming to the image the people have cherished all these years. Sreedharan's abject condition actually mirrors their own fallen state. Broken in body and mind, he reminds them of their failings, their confusion and their defeat. He forces a community in denial to confront the ugly truth they have repressed for so long. After each faction fails to buy him out, there is only one solution: to destroy the man and replace him with the original fiction they had nurtured all these years. When Sreedharan is murdered, this wish is fulfilled.

In the funeral procession that is taken out, it is the portrait of Sreedharan from 10 years ago, that of the great leader, that is borne aloft over the heads of the crowd. The camera cranes up with the portrait as it is raised, affirming the reincarnation of the man in the image. The reality of the dissolute Sreedharan is now erased from memory and replaced with this image which, ironically, serves to unite the feuding factions—at least for a day. Thus the image becomes more real than the man himself, and the entire community once again rejects reality: not only that of Sreedharan's, but also of their own failure.

"Who Is This Sreedharan?"

In keeping with the image-reality dichotomy of the film, Gopalakrishnan offers an alternate version of Sreedharan's return in the second half. In this version, his protagonist is associated with dreams and the act of dreaming. On the night he suddenly materializes from the darkness, Savithri is shown dozing, back against a wall, while Sreeni sleeps on the floor. We see her in the same room, eyes closed in an identical posture, when her father wakes her up with the news of Sreedharan's murder. We are left to wonder whether there has been any passage of time between the two scenes. Sreedharan's homecoming thus acquires the unreality of a dream dreamed by a woman who has been yearning for his return.

Gopalakrishnan employs the same idea in a slightly different form when he turns the community into a collective dreamer. This time, Sreedharan becomes the object of a wish-fulfilling dream dreamed by the people who conjure him up as an embodiment of their hopes. As Gopalakrishnan puts it, Sreedharan is the "concretization of the intense desire of a people caught in a particular historical moment."[5] But the irony lies in the fact that the man they dream into being is actually a projection of their current pathetic condition. Accordingly, instead of inventing a hero, they produce the wastrel-like Sreedharan, who exemplifies their profound despair.

In both cases, the realist foundations of the second half are suddenly undercut by these alternate scenarios, and we are invited yet again to be the arbiters of meaning. Is Sreedharan merely a figment of imagination, or does he have a concrete reality? Having reaffirmed the inadequacy of realism as a method, Gopalakrishnan retreats from the narrative and makes us the final authors of the text.

For Gopalakrishnan, all engagements with the political, within any given culture, must be undertaken with a strong, critical eye—an attitude that is self-consciously built into the film's interrogative form. It is never articulated in a formulaic way that would trivialize its significance. Instead, by repeatedly destabilizing the text and our expectations and by drawing our attention to the nature of film itself, he is able to generate an ongoing series of questions that engages us at all times. What makes *Mukhamukham* such a compelling film, then, is his construction of an open searching form in which he keeps issues alive within a deconstructive mode. While remaining culture-specific, he also avoids being trapped within the narrow, confining limits of such specificity. Instead, larger frameworks of meaning and inquiry, often philosophical in nature, are invoked.

One example of this relates to the question Gopalakrishnan poses shortly after the film begins: "Who is this Sreedharan?" It becomes a profound question that eventually transcends the film's context. We are asked to consider whether an individual can *ever* be fully grasped through any form of narrative exegesis. Sreedharan exists as a set of shifting signifiers inside the subjectivities within the film. Even with additional narratives, the film suggests, the man would remain an enigma. Reflexively, Gopalakrishnan then admits that his film can never fully explain the multifaceted truth of his subject. This, in turn, makes him focus on the image-making process itself and how the struggle to separate man from image is built into the cinema and its dichotomous relationship to reality. Since the cinema masquerades as reality, any search for the truth about Sreedharan must necessarily be premised on a lie. Even when Gopalakrishnan seeks to identify the man as distinct from the image, the latter remains, in essence, an image, accessible only on and by way of the film. The cinema has no reality except that of its unreality, which is precisely what Sreedharan becomes in the end—more real as an unreal image. The film, then, is about its own failure to explain the reality of its protagonist. Thus Gopalakrishnan's initial question—"Who is this Sreedharan?"—which is central to the film's diegesis and political content, is transformed into a complex philosophical inquiry involving the cinema as well.

At the end of *Mukhamukham*, it is hard not to feel skeptical about heroes and antiheroes, ideologies and systems, and political life in general, with all its glaring contradictions and paradoxes. Especially disconcerting is the way the community is depicted—its capacity to make and destroy the man who leads them, and what this reveals about its own deep insecurities and self-serving interests. In fact, it is pathetic to witness their collective failure to organize themselves and live up to their ideals; instead, they succumb to illusory hopes that only degrade them further. If communism offered them a concrete form of engagement with the modern and its promise of emancipation, they spectacularly fail to embrace it, making *Mukhamukham* Gopalakrishnan's most cynical and despairing film.

Chapter 2

THE DOMAIN OF INERTIA: *ELIPPATHAYAM* AND THE CRISIS OF MASCULINITY

Elippathyam (*The Rat Trap*, 1981), which won Gopalakrishnan the coveted British Film Institute Award, features men in the grip of a moral and existential crisis. It is the first of a loose trio of films that focus on a life lived within the vestiges of feudalism, the other two being *Vidheyan* and *Kathapurushan*. All three feature males from landowning families who grapple with the challenge of living in a post-feudal era where they must radically reconfigure their senses of self, identity and home. While *Kathapurushan* is a fable of affirmation and acceptance, the protagonists of *Elippathyam* and *Vidheyan* choose not to integrate themselves into the processes of history. Put differently, they refuse to budge from a space that history, with the decline of feudalism, has emptied out, but instead make a mockery of keeping the past alive. This inevitably propels them toward neurosis and even death. Instead of aligning with the forces of modernity, the men regress to states of apathy or violent excess as they cling to the remains of structures that once sustained them. Denied the material resources and legal sanctions over which their forefathers once wielded authority, they find themselves hopelessly adrift in a new and unfamiliar world. As they continue to live within the brittle, eroded foundations of their ancestral legacy, the concept of home becomes complex, unstable and paradoxically synonymous with homelessness. Their liminal existence as outsiders stuck between past and present constitutes the subject of these films. This unreal in-between space becomes the site of their psychic dislocation, which takes the form of a neurotic obsession with power that they exercise either on their immediate family members or the community at large. And yet, officially, the men have no real access to power. This strange contradiction—power within powerlessness—only confirms their perverse otherness.

Set in the early 1960s in rural Kerala, *Elippathayam* features the middle-aged Unni, who lives with his two younger sisters in their sprawling ancestral house. While Rajamaa is meek and compliant and rarely leaves the house, ministering constantly to her brother's needs, Sreedevi, in her late teens, is self-willed and headstrong. There is a third, older sister, Janamma, who, accompanied by her son, moves in with them during the film's second half. Her demand for a share of her property precipitates a crisis.

The family belongs to the matrilineal Nair community that was originally a warrior caste but later, along with the Namboodiris, became the landowning class in Kerala. According to T. J. Nossiter, the advent of Western education and the creation of a money economy, along with other social and economic factors, contributed to the erosion of their traditions in the first half of the twentieth century.[1] As the class continued to decline, the young men of the *tarawad*—joint family—were condemned to idleness and found it increasingly difficult to manage their large estates and pay for their upkeep.[2] In the film, the main sources of income are the paddy fields and coconut trees, but the yield has diminished substantially. The family can barely subsist on what is left of its inheritance.

The apathetic Unni, the sole male heir, has succumbed to a total inertia that leaves him utterly dependent on the labor of others. Rajamma works for him like a drudge, always at his beck and call while he lolls in his armchair, either reading the newspaper or sleeping for most of the day. He (still addressed as *Unni-Kunju*, which alludes to his family's elevated status) clings to an outmoded way of life that he can scarcely afford given his dwindling fortunes. A relic by choice, he has practically withdrawn from the world and refrains from virtually all forms of social interaction. Incapable of even sharing basic emotions, he exists solely within the narrow confines of his egotism. Underlying such aloofness is a fear of change and displacement. He can barely comprehend the forces outside—threatening in their alienness—that are transforming his world and that of his forefathers. Such a reclusive and indolent life, shaped by the destructive ideology of a system that has lost its historical frame of reference, generates an array of symptoms that can only be described as pathological. The film seeks to document these symptoms in the contexts of power, sexuality and labor.

For Gopalakrishnan, the central questions in *Elippathayam* are "What is being?" and "What constitutes an individual?"[3] Thus the film is not simply a study of decadence in post-feudal Kerala but has larger philosophical ramifications. Like *Mukhamukham*, it seeks to place its concerns in a universal framework without sacrificing its historical specificity. Unni's story, in this respect, is also an existential narrative about choice, entrapment, freedom and emancipation and an attempt at defining the nature of being itself.

The World of the Ancestors

The credits of the film appear on the *nalukettu*, the ancestral house, which is also the metaphorical rat trap of the film's title (the sound made by the doors is identical to that made by the trap when it is opened). The camera reveals the objects of a feudal culture—a wall clock, a Chinese jar, an oil lamp—the lifeless artifacts of the past. By singling out each object in its separateness through quick cuts, Gopalakrishnan creates a space that remains unmappable. While there are shots of a door and even a pair of keys, we only have partial access—a keyhole perspective—to the *nalukettu* during the credits. Although the camera will subsequently take us into the inner and outer realms of the house, it will refuse to create a concrete defining space that we can inhabit. We are aware of a complex of rooms, porches, courtyards and inner and outer verandahs, but of no coherent underlying plan. Even when, in the film's last section, we get a long shot of the house, it is partly obscured. Our disorientation and exclusion thus mirror those of the three characters who live an unreal existence, trapped within shifting, amorphous borders.

During the night sequences, the fluid, diffuse spaces of the house become even more opaque because of Gopalakrishnan's consistent use of chiaroscuro. Human and ghostly realms seem to overlap as the characters are swallowed up by darkness within a labyrinth. The *nalukettu*'s past, with its recurring histories and narratives, comes alive, molding lives in the present.

Unni's gradual decline is spatially represented as we see him retreat from the *poomukham*—the porch that he occupies during the day—to the interior of the mansion. In the early sections of the film, he is occasionally shown outside the house, but such instances become increasingly rare until he finally withdraws into the recesses of the *nalukettu*. The movement parallels the process of his mental collapse. In contrast, the women move out into the wider world. Sreedevi is the first to break free, and this is followed by Rajamma's departure. The solitary Unni locks himself up and hides from everyone.

Sreedevi retrieves the rat trap from the attic when the house is plagued by rats (Figure 3). Three are caught, and she "liberates" them each time by drowning them in a pond. Subsequently, the three human occupants are also liberated in different contexts. The parallels are enforced—especially in the case of Rajamma. She disappears down the same path Sreedevi takes to the pond.

Three Sisters and the Other Woman

The two sisters are carefully set apart from one another, since they embody different sensibilities and attitudes. Rajamma provides Unni with a ready supply of coffee, cooks his meals, irons his clothes and even brings him his slippers and umbrella when he is about to go out. If a cow strays into the grounds of the house, she is summoned by him to drive it out. These may not, at first, seem unusual chores performed by a sister for her elder brother until we see a pattern that repeats itself relentlessly. She puts up with all his demands,

Fig. 3. *Elippathayam.* Sreedevi carries the rat trap.

however illogical, and silently suffers the various indignities he inflicts on her. She submits to him in what is a ritual of servile obedience, disguised by domesticity and family values, especially that of filial piety. Taught to defer to her older brother, she seems incapable of stepping out of her prescribed role, even when it leaves her open to abuse. Unni degrades and reduces her to the status of a servant, but she keeps her mouth shut.

Rajamma's servility points to a deep, almost neurotic desire for some form of self-annihilation. It is partly apparent in her compulsive need to stay busy and engaged at all times. She seems to relish the grind of routine with its comforting sense of predictability and self-absorption, for it renders her oblivious to all that which is extraneous. She is repeatedly associated with cooking, grinding paste, laying out things to dry, washing dishes, drawing water from the well. These endlessly repetitive actions breed a strange and irrational sense of security. They even amount to a possible sublimation of her repressed sexual desires. If Unni has succumbed to apathy within a decadent system, she too seems indirectly a casualty of history, trapped within a dead time, resigned to a different kind of apathy. What unfolds is a profoundly tragic story of a woman's loss of humanity.

In the film's first half, Rajamma is often seen in relation to Sreedevi. The latter goes to a tutorial (for academically poor students), wears bright red *saris*, writes and receives love letters and preens before the mirror. She is not a passive victim, like Rajamma, but makes her voice heard. Strong-willed and independent, she belongs to a new generation of self-serving opportunists who can't be bothered about propriety and decorum, or, for that matter, morality. She embodies their ambitions and desire for freedom from the stifling past. While her obliging sister slaves all day, she will have almost nothing to do with the housework. She claims she is busy with her studies but fails her exams every time.

The difference between the two sisters is brought out very effectively early in the film. As Rajamma sits dejected on the porch after her brother has rejected a marriage proposal for her, Sreedevi comes home from her tutorial. The camera pans with her as she enters her room and stands smiling before the mirror. It is more than narcissism, for Sreedevi has a bevy of admirers of which she is very conscious. The sisters are thus placed in two separate spaces: one feels old and rejected and remains inert, while the other is young and expectant and associated with the moving camera. Some time later, when Rajamma squats before the oven, boiling water for Unni's bath, we see Sreedevi in her room, copying a love letter from a pulp novel. Her priorities are completely different, and, for the most part, trivial and superficial. The crosscutting associates them again with separate spaces, concerns and agendas.

Later, Sreedevi glimpses a plane in the sky and urges Rajamma to look up, but she is blinded by the sun. Sreedevi's words are revelatory: "You took your time. Do you think the plane will wait for you?" It is significant that she, not Rajamma, spots the plane, just as it is she who retrieves the rat trap and is linked to the "liberation" of the captive rats. She is also the one who will eventually break free and elope with her lover. But Rajamma's desire for freedom is never properly articulated except obliquely, because she does not quite know how to define it. Near the end of the film, alone and sick, hearing the sound of the plane, she looks for it again in vain. Both times she "misses" the flight.

The older sister, Janamma, is a large and formidable woman who likes to make her presence felt. As Unni's tormentor, she is more of a stereotype, functioning largely as a plot device to help the narrative move forward to its *denouement*. Far more interesting is Meenakshi, a low-caste laborer, who stands apart—socially and economically—from the others. She aspires toward social mobility in a changing world where class and caste lines are no longer as rigid as before. And she uses her sexuality to bypass the hierarchies that have kept her at the bottom, seeking entry into spaces that have been off-limits for her (and her people). Her goal is Unni's seduction, which would give her a much-needed social victory.

We see Meenakshi and her son trespass on Unni's property and steal from his cashew nut tree. When he catches them in the act, she drops the cloth draped across her shoulder and gives him a glimpse of her ample bosom (Figure 4). As she talks to him, smiling coyly, she fiddles with her blouse. Although

Fig. 4. *Elippathayam*. Meenakshi tries to seduce Unni.

clearly aroused by her come-on, the cowardly Unni cannot look her in the eye. For him, she represents the allure of forbidden sex, made all the more exotic because of her marginal social status. At the same time, her aggressive otherness transforms her into a sexually threatening figure who attracts and repels him simultaneously. She, in turn, tries to exploit him for her own gain, but her derisive laughter at his sexual timidity only pushes him away. When, on another occasion, she tries to disarm his fears by reminding him that she is only a woman who will not devour him alive, it has the opposite effect. The word "eat" only triggers his crippling fear of emasculation. He imagines the jaws closing in on him. His reaction also reveals his dread of outsiders, especially those who are strong and assertive. Within his self-enclosed security zone, they embody the new and the unfamiliar and, therefore, the unpredictable. The irony, of course, is that he cannot see that he too is an outsider—by choice.

In their first crucial round, Meenakshi is the winner, having invaded his physical space, generating within him both fear and longing. And this encroachment makes her want to go even farther—into the house itself. There is a scene later in the film when she approaches Rajamma in the kitchen. Significantly, she stands outside the door and looks in, asking her for some oil for her hair. When the latter obliges, she becomes bold enough to ask if she can bathe in their pond (instead of the temple pond reserved for her class). This time Rajamma is firm and says no, thus foiling Meenakshi's bid to gain access and occupy a privileged space.

All four women are placed in relation to Unni, whom they help to define as oppressor, victim and coward.

A Narcissism of the Flesh

Unni's withdrawal from the world results in an extreme form of self-absorption that translates into an obsession with his own body. The many shots of him walking, lounging in his armchair or sleeping prove how his life revolves around specific physical modes of being. These routine quotidian acts acquire a ritualistic form through repetition. Whether it is having a meal, oiling himself before a bath, or cutting his nails, they all become part of an elaborate fetishistic rite of self-love, a narcissism of the flesh. In the absence of a sex life, these acts turn the body into a site of repressed desire and its sublimation.

On three occasions we watch him minister to his body with a fastidiousness that borders on both the neurotic and the erotic.

On the first occasion, he sits on the porch and tries to snip white hair from his moustache with his scissors (Figure 5). The slow, deliberate movements of

Fig. 5. *Elippathayam*. Unni snips grey hair.

his hands and his extreme attention to detail reveal his obsessive nature. There is a cut to an enormous close-up of his finger as he inspects the strand he has extracted. It turns out to be black, so he returns to the task with renewed vigor. Hopelessly fixated with the minuscule, he seems incapable of ever stepping outside his small and exclusive physical space. The hand mirror that accompanies his compulsive preening confirms the onanistic overtones.

On the second occasion, Unni oils his body in preparation for his bath in water warmed by Rajamma. He seems almost phobic about bathing in cold water—a fear, in part, of engaging with anything that represents life's menacing rawness. Everything must be mediated and domesticated, rendered harmless and thus acceptable. Shot in long take and medium shot, we see him pace up and down, half-naked, rubbing himself indulgently with his hands. Apparently, this is another ritual that is repeated every night. In this case, the sheer physical pleasure of caressing his body acquires a particular context in relation to Rajamma who is off-screen, heating the water. Since she takes care of all his material needs, especially cooking and serving him food, she caters to his body and is a provider of pleasure. This extends to warming his bath water. As we know, all of Unni's daily rites are inseparable from Rajamma, who lives to satisfy his every whim, including, on a subliminal level, the sexual. Her presence thus inserts a subtle eroticism within the larger context of self-pleasure.

Unni's compulsive desire to stay clean underlines a need to be free from the "dirt" of the world. His few forays outside the house often feature water—washing his feet, for example, on returning home. In one instance, we see him poised uncertainly on the edge of a water-logged lane, holding his slippers in his hands, until he finally decides not to dirty his feet and turns away. Each time, we sense an almost neurotic dread of contamination. It is the old fear of things outside the self-contained *nalukettu* that causes his withdrawal. In the last section of the film, we see him reduced to an unwashed, unshaven, unkempt man who is dumped in the stagnant water of the pond where Sreedevi drowned the rats. Earlier, he resolutely refused to bathe there for fear of catching cold. Now he stands in it, shivering like a rat—a moment of supreme irony.

The scene in which Unni's relationship to his body is foregrounded for the third time is the most complex in terms of staging. We see him on the porch again, armed with a penknife, cutting his nails with exaggerated care. Rajamma was linked to the previous scene peripherally, and now Unni has to contend with Meenakshi, who suddenly shows up and aggressively asserts her presence. She brings him cashew kernels, which allude to their earlier meeting and the theft. This time, her blatantly flirtatious gestures are too much for Unni, who turns his back on her (but steals sideways glances at her). When she stands next to him, he drops his phallic knife as if stricken.

Leaving the kernels (which she takes out seductively from her waist cloth) at his feet, she departs with the taunt: "Still scared?" Exposed as a sexual coward, Unni glances at his finger and discovers that his knife has drawn blood, an obvious reference to his fear of castration. Confronted with the real thing, he is reduced to helplessness.

Unni, faced with such intimidation, channels his sex drive into the safe, non-threatening domestic ritual of dependence. The object of his attentions is, of course, loyal Rajamma. His ceaseless demands to be looked after are almost childlike but also acquire quasi-erotic overtones. Cloaked in the subterfuge of brotherly love, Unni's obsession with his sister has more than a hint of incest, but it remains unstated and, therefore, hidden. Even better, he does not have to deal with it because it exists without a name or a face, within the home, enclosed by the family, where he would like it to stay.

Power within Powerlessness

The subject of dependence provides Gopalakrishnan with a pretext to explore a related issue that is crucial to the film: labor. Unni's wealthy forefathers could afford a life of ease because they had a retinue of workers and servants at their behest. Unni aspires to such a lifestyle, but the fact that he is impoverished turns the whole thing into a farce. The yield from the land, as we know, is so small that the three of them can barely live off it.

Whatever is left of the estate is managed by Karia, whose family members were dependents of Unni's forefathers right from the feudal era. They farmed and managed the lands but never worked for wages. Karia is the last of what was once an army of retainers, and he wants to quit. As he puts it, "Let the custom die with me." His son now lives and works in one of the oil-rich Gulf states, and his money has freed them from their servile social status. Karia also complains that laborers are hard to find these days; they have learned to organize themselves and demand their rights.

With no laborers or servants to do his bidding, it seems Unni is left with only one choice: to extract labor from those near him. In this respect, the film is also a study of feudalism within the home, how it determines power relations inside the family and how it is carefully masked from within. Unni seeks to control and dominate those around him in what becomes a pitiful display of power within powerlessness. His fake assertions of authority are directed at victims who are abject like him or dare not oppose him. His put-downs only render him all the more pathetic.

Unni, invariably, turns to Rajamma, first and above all, since she provides unpaid labor (which links her to Karia) and, given her ready compliance, makes such labor perpetually available. He empowers herself at her expense, although she happens to be his sister. Thus the economic basis of feudal exploitation—of workers and peasants—shifts to the interior of the *nalukettu*. What we see is the old master-slave relationship, supplanted from the public realm to a familial one, its underlying ideology as potent as ever. The feudal mind, denied the structures that once sanctioned the abuse of power, reconfigures itself in a new social space.

For her readiness to oblige, Rajamma gets scant thanks. In fact, her efforts to please her master are reciprocated with indifference or criticism because he takes her for granted. Only when she stops serving does he take notice of her. This happens when she suddenly falls ill one morning and can't provide him with his usual morning coffee. It's the first time that his needs have not been met. When, later in the film, her health takes a turn for the worse, we see his inhuman and destructive side. He doesn't even send for the doctor and leaves her to die. He visits her only once in her sickroom, when she's completely bedridden and can't serve him anymore.

In the first half of the film, before Rajamma's health crisis, we see Unni's bid for power when he directly intervenes in her life and seeks to determine her future. It is not uncommon for an elder brother to do so for the sake of his sister's well-being, but in this case the intervention is governed solely by self-interest. We see Unni's ruthless attempt to control those who remain passive and submit to his will.

Since Rajamma is in her mid-30s and single, Kesomman, a distant relative, brings Unni a marriage proposal for her. The suitor is a widower, and, as per tradition, Rajamma would receive her share of the property at the time of her wedding. But Unni says no without a second thought, claiming their family honor would be tarnished if she were to marry a widower. Rajamma, who is listening outside the door, turns away, her hopes dashed. This is not a new scenario; each time she has lost out to her brother, who won't relinquish his faithful drudge and the property due to her.

With those who are outsiders and dare not challenge him, Unni can be even more brutal. Back home on a visit from the Gulf, Karia's son, Mathaikutty, comes to pay his respects as he would in the old feudal days. Unni ignores him at first, and then humiliates him by alluding to him as a laborer whose skin has turned black under the hot Gulf sun. But the attempt at intimidation only betrays Unni's own fears. His visitor embodies a new social mobility that he finds threatening.

Mathaikutty may still defer to him out of habit, but he's broken free from the cycle of his forefathers and made a life for himself. He even flaunts his newfound wealth by wearing flashy Western clothes. As an outsider, he represents a new world order that is synonymous with opportunity and freedom of choice—the opposite of Unni's inert, dead space.

This brief scene, then, points to the insecurity underlying Unni's manifestations of authority. As with all pretenders to power, such displays only confirm the reality of his powerlessness. Gopalakrishnan, in fact, insinuates that all feudals—whether in or out of power—are, by nature, weak and cowardly, victims of fear and guilt because they have allowed themselves to be ruled by a dehumanizing, oppressive ideology. Unni is a perverse example of this trend.

Unni's Tormentors

The second half of the film focuses on the inevitable reversal in Unni's situation as he finds himself pitted against individuals who are neither compliant nor submissive and openly challenge his fake hegemony. They are mostly members of his own family who now become his adversaries. There is a radical shift in the power game inside the house as Unni gradually concedes his powerlessness.

Since he refuses to give Janamma her share of the crop after the harvest or the property that belongs to her by right, she decides to settle the matter by moving into the house for a few days with her teenage son, Ravikuttan. Knowing full well that he is no match for her, Unni adopts his usual tactics of evasion. But his hyperactive, meddlesome nephew refuses to leave him alone, going through his things, stealing his money, even cracking the glass on his beloved torch. For a man completely engrossed in himself, the loss or "defilement" of his possessions, which empower and define him, produces a terrible sense of vulnerability. In short, Ravikuttan, egged on by his mother, becomes his uncle's invisible tormentor. Although Unni is furious, he does not confront or reprimand Ravikuttan; his explosions of anger occur privately in front of Rajamma. The simple fact is that the uncle fears his nephew and is intimidated by his brash, insolent nature, his lack of deference for his elders and his flared trousers, all of which mark him as the dreaded outsider from another generation.

With regard to Janamma, Unni refuses to be drawn into any sort of dialogue. Matters come to a head when Rajamma takes to her bed. Janamma then also becomes his tormentor, refusing to warm his bath water (while he stands waiting, covered with oil) and serving him inedible food. Unni looks at her with silent hatred but is too afraid to react. She eventually leaves with Ravikuttan, threatening to set her irate husband on him.

The other independent-minded woman in the family is, of course, Sreedevi. Like Ravikuttan, she shows no respect for her elders and couldn't care less for the traditions of the past. Thus Unni leaves her alone but soon finds himself in a situation where, as elder brother, his mediation is called for. Between the pages of an exercise book belonging to Sreedevi, he discovers a love letter. Given the moral standards of their society, a clandestine romance is cause for a severe reprimand. Unni literally sweats with anger as he reads the letter but refuses to react to the challenge, keeping the discovery to himself. One night shortly after this, Sreedevi runs off with her lover.

When Rajamma breaks the news, Unni seems initially shocked and then lapses into silence. Sreedevi's elopement is a direct slap in his face, an open rejection of his authority, but he does nothing about it. Later, Rajamma will accuse him of being totally apathetic, of not even lifting a finger to locate her. Once again, he will remain silent. This complete passivity is in direct contrast to his earlier intervention in Rajamma's life with regard to her marriage proposal. He had no compunctions then because he knew she was incapable of standing up to him.

Rajamma, unable to bear his refusal to act, finally articulates her sense of despair. She is quite ill at this point and gives voice to her deep unhappiness when she blurts out, "God have mercy on me! Take me out of this hellhole!" For the first time, she protests her abject condition and defines herself as the suffering woman. But, in the very next scene, we see her back at work, struggling to draw a bucket of water from the well. And, as usual, she brings Unni his glass of coffee. The drudgery goes on, and she seems incapable of grasping the moment's potential for change and even freedom. The tentative attempt at resistance passes even before it is properly formulated because she lacks the means to formulate it. Her reaction remains involuntary and spontaneous, incapable of being transformed through conscious mediation into concrete action. Lacking Sreedevi's shrewdness and cunning, she invariably falls back into her crippling silence. Her sickness now begins to consume her—a manifestation of her internal repressions, which finally culminate in a death wish.

Isolation and Rescue

Gopalakrishnan has spoken about how, on a complex level, *Elippathayam* is about sharing; this pertains not just to property but to "love, concerns, anxieties, fears, hopes and frustrations."[4] In its absence, one ceases to be human. Since Unni cannot step out of himself, Gopalakrishnan questions the very basis of his existence. As he remarks, "I feel that any existence in isolation from society is no existence at all."[5] Unni's life after Sreedevi's and Rajamma's departures bears this out. It is the story of his rapid decline into paranoia and is spatially represented by his withdrawal into the interior of the house. The man who used to loll on the *poomukham* in full view retreats into the inner verandah, away from the public gaze. As Janamma and her husband take matters to court and legal summons begin to arrive, Unni finds himself cornered. This time, his earlier disdain for the world is carried to its logical extreme—he simply disappears from view. But even in his hidden lair, he cannot fend off the world.

At the end of the film, Unni's situation becomes desperate. The sick Rajamma lies in her bed, barely conscious. Since he's incapable of helping her, it falls on the people of the village to rescue her. It is Meenakshi who summons the villagers and orchestrates her rescue. She's no longer the exotic sexual Other but initiates the process that will be complete with Unni's release. Her entry into the space she had coveted is now linked to a collective effort by the people that will eventually culminate in a transformative historical moment of change.

For Gopalakrishnan, these men and women who are materially impoverished with no real access to power embody a certain freedom that the neurotic Unni and his lot can never experience. In other words, they don't carry the internal scars of the depraved class that once lived off them. As he points out, "The burden of feudal heritage does not hang on them."[6] They are thus capable—among other things—of behaving more humanely toward others. Their anonymity is suggested by shots of their feet as they enter the house and carry Rajamma down the path that leads to the pond. She seems doomed to die but free at last from the suffocating trap in which she has spent most of her life.

Unni watches, passive and mute, as the villagers take Rajamma away. For the first time, he appears remorseful and guilty. When it rains later, his eyes seem to fill with tears. In this final section of *Elippathayam*, Gopalakrishnan could have turned the film into a fable of redemption through guilt, but Unni is too far gone. We watch him gradually come apart in the solitude he now embraces as he moves into the inner recesses of the house and eventually loses the ability to leave his room. The analogy with the rat in its trap is complete.

It falls once again on the villagers to intervene, but this time they take on a more symbolic role as the forces of history, exemplified by the peasantry, who occupy a dead feudal space and liberate the last relic of a decadent system. Their action thus becomes a form of protest and resistance against an entire system and its legacy, as they physically emancipate Unni by breaking down the door one night and giving him chase. He scurries around the house in panic until he is caught, taken out, dumped into the pond and left to drown. The last time we see Unni, he stands with his feet in the water, palms folded, begging for mercy. As he looks directly into the camera, he also makes eye contact with us.

However pathetic Unni may look in this closing shot of the film, the fact of his survival, for Gopalakrishnan, is in itself a source of hope and possible redemption. Out of his profound sense of loss and displacement, there could be the forging of a new attitude, even a new self. As the filmmaker explains,

"Human beings should emerge from an experience to benefit from it. Otherwise it would be a waste. He is given that chance."[7] As Unni stares at us in the final shot, we are implicated in his gaze and asked to judge whether the man is a helpless victim of a corrupt system or a vile creature. Whether he deserves a second chance that would lead to a larger spiritual emancipation depends on how we return his gaze.

Chapter 3

MASTER AND SLAVE: *VIDHEYAN* AND THE DEBASEMENT OF POWER

Made more than a decade after *Elippathayam*, *Vidheyan* (*The Servile*, 1993), based on Paul Zacharia's *Bhaskara Patelarum Ente Jeevithavum* (*Bhaskara Patelar and My Life*), also features outsiders—men in crisis—occupying a liminal space in a post-feudal world. And it too focuses on the relationship between power and powerlessness within the contexts of abuse. What has changed is the representation of such abuse. The earlier film adopted an understated poetics of symbol and metaphor, but *Vidheyan* describes, in vivid detail, the brute force with which power aligns itself to terror and violence. In fact, it is Gopalakrishnan's most graphic film in which he portrays oppression—both physical and mental—in all its intense rawness. The master-slave relationship at its center is far more venal and sordid than the one implied between Unni and Rajamma.

During the intervening years, Gopalakrishnan's vision had darkened as India's track record of social inequality and injustice had worsened with its entry into the free market economy in the early 1990s. Meanwhile, the rise of Hindu fundamentalism and the spread of ethnic and communal violence had made the problem of the Other even more acute. There is thus a new directness with which Gopalakrishnan describes the abjectness of the human condition. At the same time, the issue of transcendence acquires a new urgency, placed within the contexts of religion and faith and linked to a vision of human innocence and goodness.

Vidheyan's protagonist, Bhaskara Patelar, clings to the vestiges of a bygone era but, unlike the diffident and reclusive Unni, is a full-blown, malevolent villain who keeps a whole village in thrall. The innocent are not spared as they become the victims of some of his gratuitous displays of aggression. His well-aimed kicks send them crashing to the ground, after which he pummels them into submission with his feet. The most powerful and feared man in the village, Patelar is also known for his alcoholism and voracious sexual appetite—no young woman, married or single, is safe from his clutches.

The film is set in the early 1960s in southern Karnataka, in a village close to the border with Kerala, where Patelar's Hindu ancestors were once rich landlords and served as local chiefs. In the colonial era, they were entrusted by the British to collect taxes. Such authority soon led to the assumption of other auxiliary powers, both social and judicial. For example, the Patelars had the right to invoke the law and punish those they deemed guilty, which carried the potential for abuse and corruption. The system continued into the '60s until land legislation led to the appointment of regular revenue officials. But, as *Vidheyan* shows, power remained in the hands of those who had no legal right to it anymore. In the film, Patelar has ceased to be the headman of the village, but, for all practical purposes, his reign continues unchecked. People still defer to him as *yajamanare*—master—and cringe before him. It is the familiar paradox of the powerless remaining powerful within the enduring legacy of feudalism.

The film's credits appear over Patelar's chair and rifle, both of which stand on the porch of the local liquor shop where he holds court. His throne is conspicuous by its loss of an arm. While its decrepit condition and location establish the depraved nature of this impoverished king, the gun links him to power and violence. Patelar prefers such a public space, overlooking the village's main street, so that he can survey the world and pick his victims.

In the first half of the film, Gopalakrishnan provides us with examples of Patelar's sheer viciousness. He savagely beats up Yusuf, a rich merchant, because he happened to interrupt one of his drinking bouts. Out hunting, he rapes a woman who crosses his path. When the son of Kuttapa Rai, a well-placed villager and his young wife walk down the street, Patelar's lackeys urge him to have "some fun" with the woman. The latter hesitates only momentarily before obliging. Clearly, he has no moral scruples. He pounces on anyone he deems his prey and is feared accordingly. His victims—Kuttapa Rai and others—later seek to appease him by sending him a variety of food items.

Gopalakrishnan also depicts Patelar seated in the spacious courtyard of his house as he metes out "justice" as in the old days (Figure 6). Supplicants approach him with folded palms, either for favors or to request his intervention with regard to specific grievances. That this should happen in post-independence India, with its own judiciary, points to how an entire community remains colonized by a defunct system. Accustomed to being ruled (and abused) by their feudal chiefs, the villagers still seek Patelar's intercession and abide by his verdicts. He draws his power from their servility and fully exploits their fear and dependence. Gopalakrishnan shows this metaphorically by juxtaposing Patelar's gun with a bunch of bananas that one of the men has gifted him as a bribe.

When a supplicant complains that his wife abandoned the family and ran off with her lover (who stands, hands tied), Patelar slaps him for not being man enough to prevent her elopement. He then has the accused untied, kicks him to the ground and beats him with his feet. He spares the wife because,

Fig. 6. *Vidheyan*. Patelar dispenses justice.

as he tells her, it is shameful for a male to strike a female. Thus we witness a blatant travesty of justice dispensed in a feudal court run by a man with no legal authority of any kind. He alone determines what the law is, what the punishment should be, and carries it out in the only form he understands: violence. In this one-man legal system, the woman, in particular, has no voice at all; she is a prisoner among men, accused and abused by them. Patelar's sexist remarks only confirm the patriarchal bias of this exploitative culture.

The scene is staged in deep focus, with the predominant use of medium and long shots, to stress his performance as the male aggressor who believes in proclaiming his right to rule. In a sense, all his displays of power are performances because they have no basis in any living political reality. And yet the irony lies in the fact that the swagger and the histrionics are only too real, just like his sadism and cruelty.

What makes Gopalakrishnan's study of power-as-evil fascinating and also problematic (as we will see later) is his insistence that the vile Patelar is a victim and thus innocent.[1] We learn from the locals that he was corrupted by the "flattery" of the villagers and their ready supply of women and booze. Even if there is some truth to it, Gopalakrishnan sees him primarily as a man who is prey to the powerful impulses he was born with, acting out the compulsions he has inherited from his class and upbringing. All his actions have their source in the legacy of his ancestors, who speak through him while he does their bidding. He is thus at the mercy of forces that he cannot comprehend and that define his otherness. In this respect, the title of the film could apply to him as well.

If Patelar, then, is a victim, it does not, in any way, mitigate the heinous nature of his crimes. Gopalakrishnan is quick to condemn them as acts of evil but attributes them to a man who lacks conscience and thus has no moral compunctions. Free from the awareness of what's good and bad, he cannot rationalize the ethical implications of his deeds. He commits the crimes "impulsively," without motivation, and thus remains devoid of guilt.[2] Gopalakrishnan compares him to a child who playfully kills an ant, unaware that he can cause pain to others.[3] Such innocence is placed within a larger critique of feudalism as a system in which the sons are denied the psychology of introspection as well as any knowledge of moral standards. They thus lack the capacity to reflect on the nature and consequences of their actions and subsist without an active, living conscience.

The Abuse of Power

Since there can be no exercise of absolute power nor a diagnosis of its pathology without a victim, it is Thommie who fulfills that role in the film. A poor Christian farmer, he has moved from Kerala with his wife, Omana, and illegally occupied a few acres of land to begin cultivation. He belongs to the last phase of a series of large-scale migrations that began at the end of World War II. Peasants sold their farmlands in Kerala and crossed the border into Karnataka in the hope of finding a better life. In most cases, their hopes were dashed, and they found themselves exploited mercilessly by the Patelar village chiefs. Now a similar fate befalls Thommie.

In the film, he's associated not only with abuse and servility but also with the search for a stable living space, since "home," for him, is a precarious and fragile entity without any legal basis. The fear of eviction and being uprooted, of course, also applies to Patelar, the relic of an obsolete system, whose pretense at power also has no legal foundations. In fact, he is physically and symbolically displaced at the end of the film. Both men are thus linked to the theme of home and homelessness within their different contexts; in the case of Patelar, his eventual loss of dwelling, social status and power marks the end of his vestigial life in the post-feudal world.

Gopalakrishnan has said that *Vidheyan* is a study of "the psychology and structure of power as also an attempt to examine what lies buried beneath an obsessive servility."[4] Patelar's first meeting with Thommie is the opening set piece of the film and gives us a vivid picture of the manner in which this relationship of servility is forged. It deserves a detailed description.

Thommie is sitting in front of a shop, across from Patelar, when the latter hails him, "Come here, son of a bitch!" Thus, at the very outset, he's verbally degraded and dehumanized (he will be called "dog," "fool" and "idiot" during the course of the film). But instead of an angry or violent reaction, we see Thommie jump to his feet in terror. The camera cranes and tracks to follow him as he begins to cross the street in a stupor. It is only a few yards, but it takes an eternity. Shot almost like a ritual, what we see, in effect, is Thommie going over to the other side, an act that will transform his life utterly.

His pitiful condition is apparent as he desperately tries to cover a tear in his cotton *mundu* with one hand while his other hand hovers over his mouth in a gesture of respect coupled with fear and shame (Figure 7). Taking full advantage of his discomfiture, Patelar has him remove his hand from the gaping hole, which exposes Thommie to the raucous laughter of his lackeys. Thommie's physical humiliation now begins in earnest. When he's close enough, his tormentor aims a mighty kick at him, which throws him to the ground. As a further affront, he spits betel juice all over his face. Thommie folds his palms and begs for mercy, calling Patelar *yajamanare*. By addressing his oppressor as master, he immediately defines his servile status. After Thommie gets to his feet trembling, he's questioned about his wife: Is she young? Is she pretty? Patelar then tells him to run and shoots at him with his gun to scare the wits out of him.

Fig. 7. *Vidheyan.* Thommie awaits his humiliation by Patelar.

Thus ends Thommie's torture—except, as he discovers later, it was only a prelude to the humiliation that awaits him at home. When he reaches his shack, his wife, Omana, is sobbing inside. In Thommie's absence, Patelar has come with his goons and raped her.

It is obvious that Patelar's strategy of intimidation entails a full assault on his victim's body and mind, which only confirms his bestiality. Unleashing absolute terror, he paralyzes his prey. Physically beaten, verbally abused, covered with betel juice and shot at, Thommie is broken down into abject servility. What makes such raw aggression especially disturbing is its randomness. Patelar needs no pretext to attack and coerce obedience from a stranger, clearly relishing the sense of empowerment and control such violence generates. There's also a sadistic thrill, an indulgence in such violence for the sake of violence. With the meek and the weak, he can be especially brutal, knowing full well that they cannot retaliate.

Thommie belongs to this category, which partly explains why he readily gives in to such degradation. Physically dislocated from his native Kerala, he has become an alien within a foreign culture. Living in the margins, in constant danger of being driven out from the land he has occupied, his insecurities make him ripe for his appropriation by Patelar (who knows, as soon as he sets eyes on him, that he's an outsider, an illegal settler from Kerala). Thommie is also fully aware of his lowly economic and social status within a hierarchy based on caste, class and material power. Such a debilitating self-image, internalized long before his encounter with Patelar, has rendered him utterly vulnerable. He has convinced himself that he is dependent, servile and a foreigner—in other words, he believes in his own pathetic condition. When a "respectable" authority figure summons him, however offensively, Thommie knows he must swallow the insult and obey him. Convinced of his powerlessness, he cannot even dream of opposing him. On a subconscious level, he is waiting for such a moment to happen. In short, he is ready for enslavement. According to Gopalakrishnan, "The attitude of servility is engraved in the Indian psyche,"[5] a legacy of complex social and historical forces at work in which the politics of caste and class as well as the country's colonial heritage have played no small part. It only takes so much to trigger such a state of mind, regardless of time and place. There's also the issue of patriarchy. It is quite common for those without resources, to seek the protection of powerful male authority figures. Patelar, in this respect, conforms to the popular stereotype of the stern, disciplinarian patriarch. Thommie is only too glad to submit to this surrogate father.

The Psychology of Enslavement

As the film unfolds, servility acquires a certain trajectory in Thommie's case, culminating in the complete takeover of his self and being. During his public humiliation, his initial reaction is blind terror. When he returns home and learns of the rape, he is filled with fury and wants to hack his tormentor to pieces. In fact, he is openly defiant next day, when Patelar sends one of his lackeys to summon him. But all attempts at resistance crumble as soon as the man threatens him with eviction and worse: "How do you expect to live here?" The question cuts right to the core of Thommie's insecurity as an outsider, and he buckles under the fear of losing the ground he stands on. There is nowhere he can go if he is uprooted from his temporary and illegal home.

Thommie meekly follows the man to Patelar, who offers him a job as bartender at the liquor shop. The latter thus carves out a new space as well as an identity for him that is linked to money and that amounts to buying Thommie out. He also provides him and Omana with new clothes—the reward for their submission. From now on, their material lives will begin to improve. If Thommie's slavedom was inaugurated with verbal and physical violence, it is now paid for with a few *rupees* and in kind. If he had been made filthy with betel juice, it is now the new clothes that confirm his "clean" status. What started out as a degrading and sordid encounter is now enclosed within the respectable. The outsider has been brought into the fold and given what he seeks most—material security and the protection of a powerful local. He happily sacrifices whatever moral scruples he had along with his conscience and accepts everything gratefully. He's now officially Patelar's slave, and Omana becomes the latter's mistress with his full cognizance. He will keep his mouth shut whenever Patelar emerges from his shack after having sex with her.

To the modern mind, Thommie's acceptance and endorsement of his wife's sexual possession seems utterly revolting. And yet it is in keeping with his abject state of servility, which can only be complete when he has nothing left to call his own. This total submission, sadly, extends to his wife and the subjugation of her body. Omana's earlier violent sobbing, following her rape, displayed her profound sense of anguish as well as her helplessness. But, like him, she has no choice but to submit. And, also, like him, she gradually accepts her condition and sees no conflict in having two men share her between them. Soon, she begins to welcome Patelar's visits.

Gopalakrishnan takes the subject of threesomeness even further when he subsequently shows Omana in bed with Thommie. The latter is thrilled that his wife now reeks of Patelar's perfume—a sign that he has come to cherish her relationship with his master. It is a complex moment because a latent homoeroticism underlies it. The couple is shown in bed with Thommie embracing Omana, but it is also apparent that they are sharing Patelar between them. In *Elippathayam*, Gopalakrishnan shows how any form of suffocating dependence, which servility breeds, will invariably take on a sexual dimension. Is Thommie exempt from it? The extreme nature of his submission implies otherwise. This other attraction between the two men remains unstated in the film but is nevertheless a potent element in their lives. Thommie—in bed—vicariously experiences its power and seduction via Omana. Likewise, her presence in this scene suggests—at least on the level of the imaginary—a ménage à trois in which all three are participants in a collective erotic experience. Thus, the condition of servility transforms sexual relations and the nature of sexuality itself.

As the film develops, we see Thommie tagging along with Patelar everywhere, carrying his gun when he goes hunting, serving him liquor, and becoming an accomplice in his nefarious deeds, but all the time in fear of him (Figure 8). Gradually, there is a shift in attitude. The fear remains, but Thommie seems more at ease with the fact of his servility. After a point, he masochistically enjoys his state. As Patelar acquires a larger-than-life mystique for both Thommie and Omana, submitting to him becomes an imperative and an honor. We also notice Thommie's new devotion to his job and new loyalty to his *yajamanare*. The eagerness to please is not simply to curry favor. Serving the most powerful man in the village makes him feel strong and defines him in a way he had never experienced before. And although the unrelenting Patelar continues to abuse him verbally and physically, he no longer seems to mind. He accepts oppression as a fact of life. Eventually, such servility becomes a state of being without which Thommie seems unable to function. According to Gopalakrishnan, this ultimate

Fig. 8. *Vidheyan.* Thommie tags along with Patelar.

form of submission is the most "pathetic."[6] The servile can no longer live without the degradation he spurned earlier. More than once, Thommie exclaims that without Patelar, there would be no life for him.

Although Patelar would never say the same about Thommie, it is no secret that he depends on him completely as well. Thus, although their relationship is built on a fundamental inequality in power, it is a mutually sustaining one. After a point, neither can function without the other—especially Thommie, whose sense of self depends wholly on the bond he has forged with his *yajamanare*. This repugnant, all-encompassing nature of Thommie's servility appears to rule out any possibility of a sudden rupture. However, at times, we notice a strange duality that points to unresolved tensions within. He suddenly seems irresolute or displays feelings that suggest an impatience with the condition of his enslavement. In other words, the servile wavers in his servility. These inconsistencies are extremely revealing and, for Gopalakrishnan, signs of a repressed conscience struggling to break through.

On one occasion, when Patelar is raping a woman, Thommie slowly lifts his gun, as if in play, and then points it at his oppressor, whose back is turned to him. It seems only a momentary aberration and passes quickly, but the moment stays with us. Much later in the film, Yusuf, the victim of Patelar's irrational rage, along with other villagers, asks Thommie to assist them in their plan to assassinate Patelar. Although initially afraid, Thommie quickly agrees, displaying a sudden resolve to act against his sordid dehumanization. But the attempt fails, leaving Patelar only slightly wounded. When Thommie finds him sprawled on the ground, in front of a well, bleeding and in a state of shock, his mouth comes together, hard and bitter. For the first time, we see a look of utter hatred as well as satisfaction. Here is his chance to push him into the well and be finally rid of him. But when Patelar quickly recovers, Thommie instantly regresses to his servile state. He reaches out, helps him to his feet and weeps openly at what has befallen his *yajamanare*. He thus compromises himself hopelessly. When he escorts his master into his shack, we see the latter's colossal shadow cover most of the wall, separating Omana from Thommie. It is a powerful visual rendition of his inescapable presence in their lives, which simultaneously divides and binds them together. As she begins to weep at the sight of Patelar's bruises and Thommie looks on, the paradoxical nature of this relationship is enforced. Caught between the two, struggling to reconcile his own contradictory impulses, Thommie topples over, unconscious.

For Gopalakrishnan, these "aberrations," however inconclusive, constitute Thommie's saving grace. He portrays Thommie as a man who has allowed fear to compromise his integrity and make him servile. As Yusuf tells Thommie, "You live off Patel. But there's goodness in you. You're an innocent."

Gopalakrishnan seeks to define this goodness both concretely and symbolically within the larger contexts of faith and spirituality. Thus he repeatedly frames his protagonist in relation to religion, specifically invoking the Christian scheme of sin, suffering and redemption without, however, imposing a dogmatic reading. Instead, he intends to create a larger framework for Thommie's story of loss and rehabilitation.

Thommie is associated with a church bell as the film begins. It is a funeral bell, and we hear it as he gets up to cross the street to meet Patelar for the first time. As he is about to embrace a symbolic death, the bell tolls for him. After his appropriation by his new master, a priest complains that he neither attends church nor goes to confession anymore—a sign of his spiraling spiritual decline.

On two occasions, we see an image of Christ on Thommie's shelf at home, juxtaposed once with Omana's sobbing and, later, with the *sari* Patelar has given her. Both times we are reminded of the presence of sin and suffering in their lives—especially in relation to Omana's sexual enslavement. But the icon also offers hope for salvation.

The issue of sin also surfaces early in the film, when Thommie visits a pond within the precincts of a Hindu temple. It teems with fish that he's told "belong to the goddess" and are under her protection. Since Thommie had initially thought of catching them, he begs her forgiveness and, by way of atonement, feeds them corn and rice. We hear on the soundtrack the sound of drums, associated with Hindu worship, as the Christian Thommie offers penance to a Hindu goddess. Thommie's simple faith thus extends beyond his own religion. Although a non-Hindu, he believes in the pond's sanctity and feels real guilt for his sinful thoughts. For Gopalakrishnan, the scene affirms his innate simplicity and innocence, which make him vulnerable to coercion and exploitation but also enable him to experience the power of faith.

The pond recurs in the second half of the film as a setting for the vindication of this faith. This time, Patelar forces the terrified Thommie to accompany him there at night and help him catch the fish. He forces him to light sticks of dynamite and fling them into the water, but not even one explodes. Patelar himself tries the fifth time, but the outcome is the same. While a logical explanation would be that the sticks are damp or flawed, what matters here is that Thommie's firm belief that the fish are sacred is upheld, while Patelar, the sinner, loses out.

The Nurturer and the Mistress

For Gopalakrishnan, there is no condition—however abject—that is impervious to change. In this respect, the second half of *Vidheyan* is essentially a fable of transformation, both material and spiritual. It describes the alliance that is forged between the two men that makes them virtually indistinguishable. There is a new sense of bonding in which the categories of master and slave no longer define them as before.

The main agent of this transformation is Patelar's wife, Saroja, who appears at the end of the court scene. She stands in the doorway of their house with an anguished face as she watches her husband mete out brutal "justice." It is significant that we discover her via Thommie's gaze as he turns to look at her. A closeness will develop between these two based on their mutual unhappiness. Thommie's feelings will subsequently take the form of a quasi-erotic adoration. He even has a dream in which he sees himself with his head in her lap while she strokes his forehead. She, in turn, reciprocates—as many of Gopalakrishnan's women do—by taking on the mythic role of the nurturing mother. We see her feed him lunch with evident pleasure; he, in turn, asks her about her son as she serves him, confirming his own surrogate status.

It is Saroja who functions as Patelar's conscience (until he develops his own) by "nagging" him (as he puts it) and telling him what to do (which he resents very much). Although she loves him, she is utterly revolted at his dissolute nature and his wanton acts of violence. Whenever she learns of his atrocities, she does not hesitate to speak up. When Kuttapa Rai complains about him, she confronts Patelar with "You won't let anybody live in peace!" Nobody in the film has ever dared utter such words to his face. Saroja goes even further. Weeping loudly, she claims she would rather die than live such a life.

As the only one who can look Patelar in the eye and speak of his sins, she constitutes the most powerful moral voice in the film—urging restraint, self-control, compassion. But although she claims—with sadness—that he never listens to her, she does get through. He calls her a nag precisely because she makes him feel, for the first time, emotions, such as remorse and guilt, which disturb him. As these new emotions acquire a life and urgency of their own, he decides to stifle them by doing away with their very source: Saroja. But given his complete lack of foresight, he cannot imagine what the internal consequences will be for him. Sure enough, as soon as he gets rid of her, he activates his own conscience and finds its nagging—in the true sense of the term—unbearable. Thus Saroja's death—a symbolic death of goodness and integrity for Gopalakrishnan—begins the process that transforms him into a contrite and remorseful man who eventually seeks punishment for his sins. What is tragic is that a woman must die for the sake of a man's redemption.

In relation to Saroja, Omana comes across as the stereotypical silent, suffering woman, without any resources of her own, who depends exclusively on her husband. Like him, she too lives with an extremely debilitating self-image. Her desperate plea to Thommie is that they should stick together, regardless of what befalls them. Solidarity in the face of abject humiliation and servitude is their only chance for survival.

The most distressing aspect of Omana's life is, of course, her sexual enslavement by Patelar. The night of her rape, Thommie stands outside, listening to his wife's sobs, while the camera holds onto the doorway and the room beyond in a medium shot. By excluding Omana from the frame (we have not seen her yet), Gopalakrishnan links her metaphorically with both the empty space (her terrifying inner void) and the threshold that confines her (her virtual imprisonment as a woman). She will, at first, be almost exclusively associated with these tropes of invisibility and absence, and since she speaks only a few words in the film, her off-screen crying voice will complement her often ghost-like presence. Thus Omana is conceived as the marginalized female who is exploited economically, socially and sexually, and who is incapable of resistance. The only sources of hope in this devastating scene are the flickering lamp and the image of Christ on the shelf, but they seem about to be engulfed by the surrounding darkness.

Ironically, the man who frees her from her insubstantiality is Patelar; he gives her a certain identity and importance that she begins to find empowering. Although this happens within the degrading context of her sexual bondage, the repercussions are profound. Her initial submission to Patelar was prompted by her sense of helplessness, but fear and loathing are gradually transformed into their very opposites. Like Thommie, she goes through the successive stages of humiliation (she wants to kill herself), anger, acceptance and empowerment. She also—pathetically—comes to enjoy her situation as her oppressor becomes her lover and master. As the mistress of the most powerful man in the village, she begins to look forward to his frequent nocturnal visits. Thus husband and wife parallel each other in their descent into abject servility.

Unlike Gopalakrishnan's other female protagonists, Omana finds herself locked into a triangular relationship where she must satisfy two men at the same time. In the "threesome" sequence discussed above, although Thommie claims she belongs to him alone, both know this is no longer true. The solidarity they had upheld as husband and wife has been transformed with the inclusion of a third person. Her sense of belonging has become complex and problematic. Taught to love and serve her husband, she must now cater to another man with her husband's tacit approval. That she has to depend on or belong to either one or both is, of course, unfortunate, but she's incapable of breaking free. Meanwhile, the threesomeness provokes the larger question of divided loyalties. After Patelar's attempted assassination, we see Omana break down and weep at the sight of his wounds, thus displacing Thommie from his place as husband and man of the house. Later, in the final section of the film, Patelar who is on the run, comes to their shack and asks Thommie to accompany him. Omana breaks down again, but this time her tears are for her husband, at the inevitability of their separation. She is thus trapped in an extremely challenging and difficult situation, grappling with the complex emotional (and sexual) demands made on her by two very different men. Because she cannot choose between them, she must accept and accommodate them both in her life.

The Awakening of Conscience

In the murder plot he hatches, Patelar makes Thommie his accomplice, despite his protestations. He intends to shoot Saroja as she serves the latter a glass of rice water and make it look like the gun went off accidentally. It is very important, Patelar tells Thommie, that she must not suspect that her husband was behind it. As he puts it, "She must not die with that grief." Patelar's sudden concern for her thoughts and feelings at the very moment of her death is new and startling. While he has no qualms about killing her, what she may *think* suddenly matters to him profoundly. The attempt is botched when Patelar fires, misses Saroja, and shoots Thommie instead. As the man lies critically wounded, she (unaware of the plot) overrides Patelar's objections and sends him to the hospital. Later, when he is recuperating at home, she visits him with a basket of provisions (as per her role of nurturing mother), which triggers his dream. Having taken the bullet meant for her, although not intentionally, Thommie has proven the depth of his attachment, and the wound is symbolic of how much he cares for her. She, in turn, saves his life by sending him to the hospital.

Patelar's second attempt succeeds, but he keeps Thommie out of it. He enters through the bedroom window, his head covered with a towel, and strangles Saroja. Although she does not see his face, she manages to grab both his hands. After breaking the news to Thommie, Patelar asks him to make the murder look like a suicide by hanging. In the scene that follows, Thommie breaks down and weeps inconsolably, holding onto Saroja's feet as she dangles from the ceiling. His sense of personal loss is compounded by the feelings of guilt and betrayal that he has harbored since the first attempt on her life. He finally lets it all out.

Saroja's death affects Patelar as well. He now seems obsessed with only one thing: the possibility of his wife having recognized him when she caught hold of his hands. He asks Thommie for corroboration, then tries to reassure the dead Saroja: "I didn't kill you. It was an accident." Later, he shines his torch into Thommie's face and asks, "Can one tell a person by touching the hands?" When Thommie replies he doesn't know, Patelar has him touch his hands and asks, "Is it me?" This time Thommie says yes, instead of catering to his *yajamanare* as he has always done in the past. Patelar is left on his own to grapple with his guilt. This is probably the first time that he has sought Thommie's opinion as well as directly solicited his physical contact. Both mark the beginning of a new relationship between them. But for the present, Thommie has confirmed Patelar's worst fears of being recognized by Saroja. His conscience is now not only wide awake but in torment.

Following Saroja's murder, Patelar finds himself on the run, pursued by her brothers and the police. The people of the village also join forces to depose their tyrant once and for all. Although their presence in the film, as in *Elippathayam*, has been peripheral, they symbolize the forces of resistance against their old foe and, like the people in the earlier film, sweep away the last vestige of a cruel and oppressive system.

When Patelar shows up at Thommie's house one night, he is a changed man, physically and otherwise. Bearing the external and internal wounds of the violence he has suffered, he is now a victim of abuse like Thommie. Stripped of all his possessions and dressed only in a *mundu*, he resembles the latter outwardly. He even sits on the floor like Thommie and eats the same food.

The correspondences between the two begin to intensify. On a certain level, this is an offshoot of their old dependence, since one defined and sustained the other. However, their roles were carefully demarcated within the hierarchy of power. Now, with Patelar a wanted man, that hierarchy is no longer fully functional. While no conspicuous role-reversal occurs in the sense that Thommie becomes the dominant partner, there is, for Patelar, a symbolic going over to Tommie's side. Beaten, humiliated and rendered completely vulnerable, the oppressor has become the oppressed and vicariously shares his condition. He is now as much victim and outsider as Thommie, and his conscience continues to assail him over Saroja's death.

At this stage in the film, the men are no longer partners in sin but have broken free from their master-slave bondage into true interdependence, which will eventually have a positive outcome. It will enable them, among other things, to access a new and complex sense of freedom. In Patelar's case, this freedom will be, in the end, associated with death as the ultimate redemptive liberation.

When Patelar, looking for a hideout, visits Thommie at night, he asks Thommie to come with him. It is not so much an order as a request, and he offers Omana money as recompense. The scene is meant to remind us of the one in which Patelar—also bruised and bleeding—cast his huge shadow on the wall after the attempt on his life. This time Omana weeps again, but the tears are not for Patelar; they are for Thommie, at the prospect of their separation. The latter, instead of comforting her, regresses into his servile mode and claims, "I'm there for the master." She is thus relegated to second place.

The scene points to the need for Thommie and Omana to free themselves from the shadow of their oppressor and revive their old relationship of love and trust.

Taking Thommie with him, Patelar now heads into the jungle, the last refuge of the outsider. In these closing minutes of the film, nature becomes a significant presence. As they go deeper into this elemental world, they rely on their basic survival skills and subsist on the little food they carry with them. Although Thommie is obsequious to Patelar as before, there is a subtle leveling of differences. This is especially true of Patelar as he becomes even more aligned with his victim in these final scenes. In long shot, we see them both drink from the river in almost identical postures. Later, both eat from the same food packet, something which would have been unthinkable in the past. When Thommie goes to have a wash, the camera moves slowly to Patelar, who sits staring at the rice boiling in the pot as if this is now his priority. His posture—in long shot—resembles Thommie's in the opening scene of the film.

Finally, Patelar calls Thommie by name. Accustomed to verbal abuse, the latter is profoundly flattered to discover he has suddenly acquired an identity. When Patelar asked him to touch his hands, he began dismantling the hierarchy that kept them apart. Calling him Thommie is further evidence of this process. Patelar now repeats the question that won't let him rest: "Would Saroja have recognized me?" This time, Thommie plays the ingratiating servile and says no. But his master is not convinced. Words cannot help him anymore, and his guilt translates into a longing for some form of retribution.

Saroja's brothers have hired gunmen who pick up Patelar's trail and track him into the jungle. As their shots ring out, Patelar tries to flee, then stops and slowly lifts his gun above his head in a gesture of surrender, his posture and wounds making him a potential Christ figure. Thommie was earlier placed in relation to Hindu penance; in Patelar's last moments, he is linked to Christian ideas of redemption. When shots are fired again, he slumps to the ground beside a roaring waterfall. No longer seeking escape, he submits to his death as a form of atonement and release. Such a violent end has a certain logic and even necessity in relation to him; it also frees the community that has lived in fear of him.

At first, Thommie is extremely distraught and weeps over the corpse of his *yajamanare*. So deeply entrenched is his servility that he cannot even fully comprehend that he is finally free. After he calms down, he picks up Patelar's gun and flings it into the river, severing all ties with the past and his life of degradation. Gopalakrishnan cuts to a medium shot of the waterfall, which, appearing at the end of a narrative of profound internal and external discord, is deeply cathartic, an image of transcendental splendor.

As Thommie runs home to Omana, crying out, "The master is dead," we hear church bells. It is not the tolling of the funeral bell as at the start of the film this time, but a call to the congregation. It rings for Thommie as a vindication of his new birth and his reintegration into the community he had shunned. One could also read into this joyous calling a specific Christian allusion to Thommie finding grace after his long and terrible ordeal, but such a reading in not imposed on the film.

Vidheyan ends with the camera leaving Thommie and panning to a shot of distant hills while the bells continue to chime. This landscape, bereft of all human contexts, places the film and its events beyond the comforts of religion and all man-made systems. It brings closure to the human drama after all its material and spiritual possibilities have been exhausted and even nature has ceased to be a redemptive presence. The pan (and the earlier shots of Thommie running) foreground movement and the idea of an ongoing quest into a greater space that enfolds the visible world but also extends beyond it.

This moment of "natural" transcendence at the end is more convincing than Gopalakrishnan's attempt to cast Patelar as a Christ-figure complete with stigmata, reiterating his innocence and, especially, his status as victim. Having witnessed the nature and extent of the evil Patelar commits in the film, it is very difficult for us to accept his actions as those of an unthinking innocent or see him merely as slave to a social system that has taken over his mind. Such a representation is incompatible with what history teaches us; oppression originates from conscious and deliberate patterns of choice and motivation. Even if some of Patelar's villainy could be attributed to his feudal legacy, his actions demonstrate will and purpose and an ability to distinguish between good and evil. He's canny and shrewd and takes advantage of every opportunity from which he can derive some personal gain. He's also fully cognizant of the pain he causes others. Thus he cannot be absolved from his personal responsibility for his crimes. In short, the claim for his innocence as well as his transformation into a surrogate Christ has almost no foundation in *Vidheyan*.

What *is* strong and credible in the film is Patelar's sense of guilt, stemming from Saroja's murder, and the process by which he is transformed. Dissolute men *can* experience feelings of regret and remorse that lead to expiation and possible redemption. A compelling case is made for Patelar in this regard, and one wishes Gopalakrishnan had stopped there instead of trying to free his protagonist from all charges of personal culpability.

The reiteration of innocence applies to Thommie as well. While his tragic story of abuse, servility, and emancipation acquires its own internal logic, we are not allowed to forget, lest we miss the point, that the man is essentially good and a victim of circumstance. Such an insistence is eventually counterproductive because it compromises his individuality and encourages us to see him as a certain type or symbol. It also simplifies the nature of his conflicts where innocence, at all costs, must be vindicated. What is far more compelling is how Thommie exceeds Gopalakrishnan's attempts to define and limit him and asserts his own uniqueness as a complex individual in his own right. In a narrative of oppression and enslavement, such an affirmation of independence from the strictures of the text and the filmmaker's preconceived agendas may perhaps constitute the ultimate freedom.

Chapter 4

THE SERVER AND THE SERVED: *KODIYETTAM* AND THE POLITICS OF CONSUMPTION

Kodiyettam (*Ascent*, 1977) is set in the 1970s, at a time when the Nehruvian dream had floundered in India and there was widespread discontent in the country. The 1964 split in the Communist Party along with the failure of political reforms in Kerala had led to a loss of faith in all governmental institutions and state-sponsored initiatives. But other than a few cursory references to political rallies and the expulsion of a Party member, the film makes no allusion to the events that were being hotly discussed and debated. Instead, Gopalakrishnan focuses on a village in Kerala where an unrepentant, regressive patriarchal culture has turned its back on modernity and all forms of progressive reform. Shaped by the legacy of feudalism, it is a culture of wasteful self-indulgence and degrading *machismo*. The men live suspended in a time-warp, outside all norms of productive social living—a community of outsiders. They are repeatedly associated with mindless consumption and a demeaning corporeality that symbolizes their depraved form of otherness. Some are callous fathers and husbands; others cheat on their wives. A few have short fuses that ignite suddenly and unpredictably. Most of their pathetic displays of power are directed at women. Emotionally and morally stunted, these men blindly subscribe to an oppressive ideology of self-serving excess.

Gopalakrishnan's critique of masculinity, then, is directed at an entire culture, a whole way of life. Since the people in the film are incapable of any collective form of redress, he invests in the individual's potential for emancipation and makes him a symbol of hope for the community at large. His protagonist, Sankarankutty, is an orphan in his early thirties who clings to an infantile state, refusing to grow up and become a man (as his mother-in-law subsequently laments). In relation to the other males, his symptoms are relatively minor, but they can be traced to the same malaise that has infected them all. Compared to these men, he is merely simple, foolish and naïve. Not even remotely interested in finding a job, he lives off his sister Sarojini's earnings (she works as a maid in the city and sends him money), which fuel his massive eating and drinking bouts (Figure 9). He is thus at the center of the film's complex discourse on the body, expressed through the tropes of food, feeding and gluttony.

The story of Sankarankutty's transformation from a quotidian state to that of a full-fledged adult, husband and father occupies most of the film. Gopalakrishnan calls him a "floating" character who "starts asking questions and, in the process, slowly becomes an individual."[1] In other words, he has not lost his ability to evolve and can thus separate himself from the faceless

Fig. 9. *Kodiyettam*. Sankarankutty and Sarojini.

masses around him. What we have, in effect, is a narrative of self-growth built around the question, "What does it take to be a man?" This question, of course, applies to the community as well. Sankarankutty's success offers them the chance—whether they grasp it or not—to reconfigure their priorities and perhaps redeem themselves from their animalistic state.

Kodiyettam is also the study of a marriage and the attempt to build a home. Sankarankutty's marriage to Santhamma generates a profound crisis in his life because of the limits it places on his freedom. Never before has he faced the challenge of being responsible for somebody else or sharing a space that belonged solely to him. Rather than deal with it, he displays a compulsive need to flee that manifests from time to time. In short, he simply runs away from home like a truant boy, without bothering to inform his wife. These escapades gradually erode the foundations of their marriage and eventually destroy the home Santhamma has sought to create. Thus the familiar tropes of displacement and dislocation in relation to home and family reappear in *Kodiyettam*.

Gopalakrishnan's allusions to food and consumption are a way of documenting the shifts within the marriage he depicts. The relationship between the couple is examined largely in terms of who serves food to whom and what the psychological, social and cultural implications of such a ritual are. In doing so, Gopalakrishnan unravels the power politics of what is given and taken, what is lost and gained—in short, what is at stake for two people who engage in something as basic as filling their stomachs. A brief account of the ritual is necessary here.

The Ritual of Feeding

In virtually all of Gopalakrishnan's major films, we encounter the following scenario: a man squats on the floor devouring food served by a woman who sits across from him. On display is the material and sensory gratification of the body via the act of eating, which often borders on gluttony. The cook is invariably the woman, defined in the nurturing role of provider to the man who consumes her meal. She is thus cook, provider and server all rolled in one.

Within Kerala's traditional society, the mother always cooks and serves the son until he marries and his wife takes her place. Both cooking and serving, for the man, are thus feminized from the outset, with women firmly tied to the act of nourishing and providing for the male. A well-cooked meal is, of course, a feast for the senses, and with the mother as server for the male child, the notion of pleasure is inextricably linked to the maternal. When subsequently the man's wife becomes the provider, the pleasure of eating is conflated for the male with both the maternal and the sexual.

Typically, the man sits on the floor and waits to be served. He then bends his body forward to reach for the food and transfers it—rolled up in his fingers—to his mouth. The woman usually sits across from him, replenishing his plate and watching him eat. The gaze is thus very much part of the ritual. Although they are spatially equal—both on the same floor—the woman remains within her separate space. What's more, she does not eat with him. There is thus no context for sharing or any form of exchange in what is basically a one-sided ritual. She usually eats alone or with other women in the house after the man finishes his meal and exits the room. As patriarchal values began to infiltrate Kerala's matrilineal society, the notion of being served and fed by a woman gradually acquired undertones of privilege and entitlement for the male. This sense of empowerment would be confirmed and articulated within other contexts of male hegemony as well.

As we watch men gorge themselves on the food their women provide, we are asked to critique the nature of this ritual. It becomes a microcosm of their unequal power relations. As Uma da Cunha observes, "The only communication between husband and wife can be the serving of food. The rest is then silence or suffering, unless the wife becomes less a servant and more a person."[2] In *Kodiyettam* the survival of Sankarankutty's marriage depends on whether the couple can reconfigure their roles and the woman can indeed break out of her silence. Accordingly, Gopalakrishnan includes both gendered points of view, that of the server and the served. He shows us how the ritual is defined, challenged and rejected, only to be reinstated within a new set of circumstances. He also makes the woman a pivotal figure who resists her complete absorption into a relationship that could rob her of her humanity.

The first time we see Sankarankutty eat a substantial meal is under the happy gaze of Kamalamma, a widow with a young son. He does odd jobs for her—chopping wood, whitewashing her house—and she feeds him after the work is done. She thus pays him for his services in food as part of an unstated economic transaction. But Kamalamma's gaze complicates matters. As she watches him break up a block of wood with his axe prior to the meal, she seems to slip into a reverie. Her point-of-view shots reveal a near-naked youthful body, muscles rippling, sweat pouring under the hot tropical sun. The meal she cooks for him, Gopalakrishnan insinuates, is more than just a token of gratitude.

The sequence consists mostly of tightly framed medium shots of Sankarankutty and Kamalamma that keep them together in the frame and yet set them spatially apart. In these two-shots, she typically sits across from him and replenishes his plate, looking at him affectionately as he devours her food. Her gaze is, on one hand, the fond maternal gaze; she symbolically occupies the place of the mother. But there is a difference. The proximity of her body to his, the joy she derives from watching him eat and the joy he derives sampling her cuisine all generate a certain sexual feeling in the scene. In fact, what she offers him, in essence, is pleasure with the unspoken hope that it will be reciprocated in kind. But Sankarankutty seems oblivious to her overtures as she puts out a variety of dishes before him. The appeasement of *his* body is clearly his first and foremost concern. What he also relishes, egotistically, is her gaze, which empowers and makes him feel special. When Kamalamma asks if he is planning to remain single, his shy smile as he looks up into the camera displays either a lack of awareness or a refusal to grapple with the subject she is trying to broach. To be single and unattached is also to be free from all obligations, which is what Sankarankutty cherishes. As long as Kamalamma sits across from him, ensconced in her own space, all is well.

Kamalamma's son now materializes as if on cue to this discourse on conjugality, and, by implication, procreation. We see him come home from school and immediately ask for food while his mother chides him for being impatient. Such impatience—however "innocent" and directed at his mother—points to how he already subscribes to a male culture that demands that women nurture them with food, sex and other pleasures while sacrificing their own desires and expectations.

Gopalakrishnan subtly reinforces the maternal aspect within this archetypal feeding scene by showing the two male "sons" eating together, side by side, while Kamalamma mothers them. A subsequent shot-reverse-shot pattern reveals the boy grinning as Sankarankutty contorts his mouth while chewing. They seem equals in age and disposition. Thus the scene closes with an element of playfulness but does not distract us from the crucial equation of the maternal with the sexual that Gopalakrishnan has so skillfully established with regard to Kamalamma and Sankarankutty.

When Sankarankutty's sister, Sarojini, comes to visit him shortly after, we see the same feeding ritual repeat itself, but with variations. Her association with the food theme is evident as soon as she enters the film because her brother is busy felling coconuts. When it is time for her to leave, her parting words allude to the fish and rice she has prepared for him. Thus their relationship is bracketed by references to food.

Sarojini is shown cooking, framed by the doors of the kitchen—a room Sankarankutty never enters in the film. He stands outside this female sanctum and asks for his lunch with the full prerogative of the impatient male we encountered earlier. And she is quick to oblige. With her back to the kitchen, she sits on the floor and, like Kamalamma, ladles food on his plate and smiles as she watches him dig into it. Since he has been drinking, he belches as she serves, but instead of reprimanding him, she alludes to it with good humor.

The fact that Sarojini is a physically attractive woman with a certain sex appeal is not lost on us. At the very start of the sequence, she is linked to the oil sputtering in the pot as she sprinkles seasoning on it. Her body bends seductively when she serves. Once again, there is the sort of frisson that was apparent in the scene with Kamalamma, except that the feeling is now more sensual than sexual. It reinforces the context of pleasure and eroticism that a sumptuous meal served by a beautiful woman will conjure up for the self-serving male.

Sarojini's presence in this scene also points to the fact that she provides for him materially, sending him money from her wages. The meals she cooks have their source in her earnings. Here too, then, is an unstated economic context, and we wonder why she does not simply stop supporting him and make him do something with his life. But as younger sister and woman, she defers to him, knowing full well the codes that prescribe her behavior, even when the man in question is her brother. We wonder whether her meekness also stems in part from the fact that she works as a maid, where deference is the norm. The theme of the server as servant could be applied literally and metaphorically to Sarojini who, in her professional life, is just that.

When it is time to replenish Sankarankutty's plate, Sarojini tells him, pot in hand, that she has contacted a matchmaker and would like to find him a wife. The fact that both women bring up the issue of Sankarankutty's marriage while they feed him seems more than just a coincidence. Given the spatial setting, each knows that they inhabit the space that once belonged to his mother and should now rightfully belong to his wife. Accordingly, they conceive of his spouse in the role of provider. Having fully internalized the stereotype, they apply it to another woman without a moment's hesitation. Sankarankutty stayed silent earlier, but his response to Sarojini is a belch—his crude way of asserting his singlehood and his freedom, which, among other things, allows him to drink whenever he pleases.

Marriage and Escape

It is only appropriate that the next important allusion to food is made when the reluctant Sankarankutty accompanies Sarojini's matchmaker to inspect Santhamma. He's asked to take a look at her as she, significantly enough, milks a cow (its off-screen mooing acts as a refrain all through the scene). She is thus immediately equated with the animal and the nurturing metaphor through which her worth is gauged by the men. What remains to be determined by them before she is fully confirmed in her role as provider is the quality of her cooking.

When Santhamma's mother announces that lunch is ready, she is thinking along the same lines, because her daughter's culinary feats will hopefully seal this important transaction. Sankarankutty can hardly wait, and he is joined by the matchmaker on the floor. Since it would be unseemly for the daughter to serve the men on this occasion, the job falls to the mother. Santhamma can only peep at them from behind the door. Gopalakrishnan, typically, focuses on the gendered gaze, contrasting her surreptitious spying with Sankarankutty's earlier brazen, objectifying look. What aligns them, however, on both occasions, is the context of food and nurturing. When he belches loudly at the end of the meal, she can barely suppress her mirth and thus fails to register his ominous, unrepentant self-indulgence.

Replete with food, Sankarankutty falls into a doze. When the matchmaker inquires—in the mother's presence—whether he approves of the girl, he is jolted out of his stupor and, without even thinking, blurts out, "Yes." If he had been awake, he would probably have evaded the question, but a full stomach decides for him that he must marry Santhamma. Her cooking has won the day.

There is a direct cut to her, now married, in Sankarankutty's kitchen. The moo of a cow off-screen revives the earlier nurturing metaphor. Our first glimpse of her as spouse is thus fittingly as wife-cook. While she sits on the floor like Sarojini and stirs the pot, he sleeps. When she nudges him gently, he happily slumbers on. Having decided to make him some tea, she busies herself again in the kitchen. When she returns to his room, minutes later, with a glass in her hand, he has vanished. Being there and not being there—this is precisely how his relationship with Santhamma will now evolve. There will be more sudden departures and disappearing acts, some of which will stretch into days and weeks. The sequence ends with the moo of the cow, as if to underline how she is hopelessly trapped in her newfound role. She's expected to give selflessly but expect little or nothing in return.

As she looks for him standing in the doorway, Gopalakrishnan cuts to a close-up of a big steaming kettle sitting on the oven at the local tea shop. This is one of Sankarankutty's haunts, where he joins the locals for gossip, banter and food. The owner reluctantly obliges him, reminding him each time that his dues are mounting. In this all-male world, there is no nurturing and no maternal providers of any sort. Money rules all transactions. It is here that we discover Sankarankutty sipping tea on credit.

His escapade may seem puzzling at first until we realize that accepting Santhamma's proffered hand would mean assuming her responsibility as husband, a role he is still not ready to embrace. Her tea does not cost him anything but entails a larger emotional and moral price, which he refuses to pay. In this sense, paradoxically, the food and drink he samples at the shop are "free." Here he can also feel happy and unencumbered within the comforting anonymity of men.

When he finally returns home, it is night. His neighbors have given his wife company and, as they leave, one of them chides him for being irresponsible. Santhamma could have taken the cue and berated her husband, but instead becomes the submissive wife and apologizes for having informed the neighbors. The scene is shot mostly from her perspective as she occupies the elevated porch, with Sankarankutty below her, dimly lit. She is spatially in a position of power but refrains from exercising it while he stands before her, head down, looking guilty. Instead, she asks whether she should serve him dinner, and he immediately agrees with a smile. Thus their reconciliation is effected through food. There is a tacit assumption that he has won the first round as their traditional roles are reconfirmed. But will she continue to play the compliant wife who will make no demands but simply cater to her husband's needs? What follows is a deviation from the script.

In the following scene—almost wordless—we see Santhamma, for the first time, take Kamalamma and Sarojini's place. She serves Sankarankutty and watches him eat, but the fond gaze is replaced by a worried look. There are cuts from him gorging on the food to close-ups of her concerned face as she tries to read the man before her. The ritual thus undergoes a reconfiguration. She is still the provider, fulfilling her role, but is consumed by a feeling of unease.

Sankarankutty, his face sharply divided into light and shadow, squirms under this new, alien, searching gaze. He rarely looks up at her but escapes into what becomes an orgy of eating. There are graphic shots of him stuffing himself with such ardor that he sighs more from exhaustion than pleasure. A nervous energy bordering on desperation characterizes his movements, while the camera cuts frequently to the frowning Santhamma sizing him up. Under such surveillance, there is no way out except through food. In terms of duration, this is the film's longest sequence that focuses on the sheer physical act of eating.

When she asks him if he has been drinking, he is quick to admit to it. There is no sly exchange of smiles as with Sarojini nor any belches that would be forgiven. She leaves the matter there but succeeds in making him feel that his privileges as male are slipping away. For the first time in his life, he is pitted against a woman who may not defer to him next time, who is stronger in every way and who will not mind making it known. What is more, she refuses to play mother to him, thus wrecking his expectations of maternal indulgence. When he demands more rice, she reveals that the pot is empty. Gopalakrishnan cuts to a high angle wide shot in which Sankarankutty, now on his feet, occupies the foreground of the frame, while Santhamma is in the rear, with the pot between them. It is his moment of truth, and he has not bothered to find out if there is any food left for her. Although he looks suitably abashed, he is powerless to act, appearing small and diminished in the near-darkness of the room. What he hates has come to pass: being embroiled in other people's affairs, having his independence compromised and being made to feel guilty. Thus, if Santhamma's initial feeding overture led to the restoration of the status quo—however shaky—in terms of power and hierarchy, now the absence of food at the end of the sequence brings them both back to a place of uncertainty and ambivalence. It is as if they have to start all over again.

So far, the female providers we have met have all been indulgent and accommodating. With Santhamma, we see a shift as she begins to question her role and status as woman and wife-mother. In the above sequence, her sacrifice and self-denial made her part of another popular stereotype: the wife who feeds her husband but is happy to go hungry, content as long as he's content. She will resolutely fight such a stereotype in the face of Sankarankutty's almost complete indifference to her needs and desires. Unlike the other women, she will not simply accept her role as provider but tap into the power that comes with it. The ritual of feeding will, accordingly, change in radical ways.

Gopalakrishnan glosses over the details of Sankarankutty's next escapade. We see Santhamma on the porch at night, this time without her neighbors, but she is not the only one waiting for him. Sivan Pillai, a notorious alcoholic, is also there. Sankarankutty finally shows up but refuses to accompany his old drinking buddy to the liquor shop. Clearly, it is in deference to his wife's presence and anxious gaze. This small victory empowers her enough to openly voice her resentment for the first time after the man has left. She speaks, as before, standing on the porch while he's below. Framed in a low angle shot, she looms over him while he remains silent and passive. She is completely fed up, she exclaims, with a loafer like him, who returns home only at night. When he does not react, she tells him sharply that his dinner is ready and that he should help himself. If she went without food for his sake on the last occasion, it is now done in protest. The server, in other words, chooses not to serve him or herself. She thus rejects the role of the self-sacrificing wife and redefines herself as the provider who will function only within a context of mutual caring and reciprocity. In other words, the husband too must become a provider. But Sankarankutty, although chastened, offers her no words of apology or comfort. Instead of heading to the kitchen for his solitary meal, he follows her into the bedroom and lies down beside her as she cries profusely. This is the only gesture he makes. Its import remains ambiguous because he makes no subsequent attempt to mend his ways. With no recourse to the ritual that night, they go to sleep hungry and, thus, achieve an equality as two bodies deprived of both physical and emotional nurturing.

Sankarankutty disappears for several days. Resigned now to his absences, Santhamma does not react angrily at first but offers him sarcasm on his return

(Figure 10). But when he yawns and stretches his body languidly on the porch, it is too much for her, and she berates him for being a "shameless man" who refuses to change. She has suffered enough, she tells him, and cannot take it anymore. We then find out that Santhamma is pregnant and wants to go home for the sake of her child. The scene ends without a single reference to food or eating. The ritual of feeding, with all its inherent symbolism, has been completely abandoned with the death of all conjugal feeling.

At the same time, the scene does contain an unstated allusion to food; Santhamma's body has become the natural provider for her child. In this new role as mother-to-be, she can stand outside the demands and stereotypes imposed on her by men. It is a deeply empowering feeling, to be free from their self-serving version of her as provider. She can now inhabit her own space as woman and mother and become a provider on her own terms. The desire to return home to her mother and to a nourishing female space underlines this awareness.

The next time we see Santhamma, Sankarankutty has been away for two weeks. She sits on the porch, shredding and consuming tapioca (which she eats uncooked to satisfy her craving, as a pregnant woman, for raw food). When someone inquires about him, she speaks of his absence almost laconically, as if it is only to be expected. Her husband's periodic disappearances have become a fact of life. As she eats, the metaphor of her body as food—food for her child—is invoked once again. Within her self-contained nurturing world, Sankarankutty has no relevance. When he eventually returns home, it is too late; she has already left with her mother.

This is the turning point in the film, for we now witness the process by which Sankarankutty becomes a man in order to win back his wife (and child). For Gopalakrishnan, it begins with the onset of guilt and remorse (however inchoate) and a display of concern for Santhamma (although this feeling did not stop him from running away from home). Even though his old freedom and independence have been restored after her departure, things are not the same. Besides, the village gossips have branded him a weak, spineless male abandoned by his wife. He must reclaim his public image.

Sankarankutty makes the trip to Santhamma's village, but things go badly from the outset. His mother-in-law cannot bear to see him and delivers the ultimate insult by questioning his manhood: "Are you a man?" And Santhamma, from inside the house, declares she has no husband. Thus his identity comes apart as he is denied his sex (in what amounts to a symbolic castration by the mother) as well as his marital status. In deep crisis, he steps inside, hoping to persuade Santhamma to come home. He gets to see his child for the first time, but the cloth cradle stands between him and his wife as a line of division that excludes him.

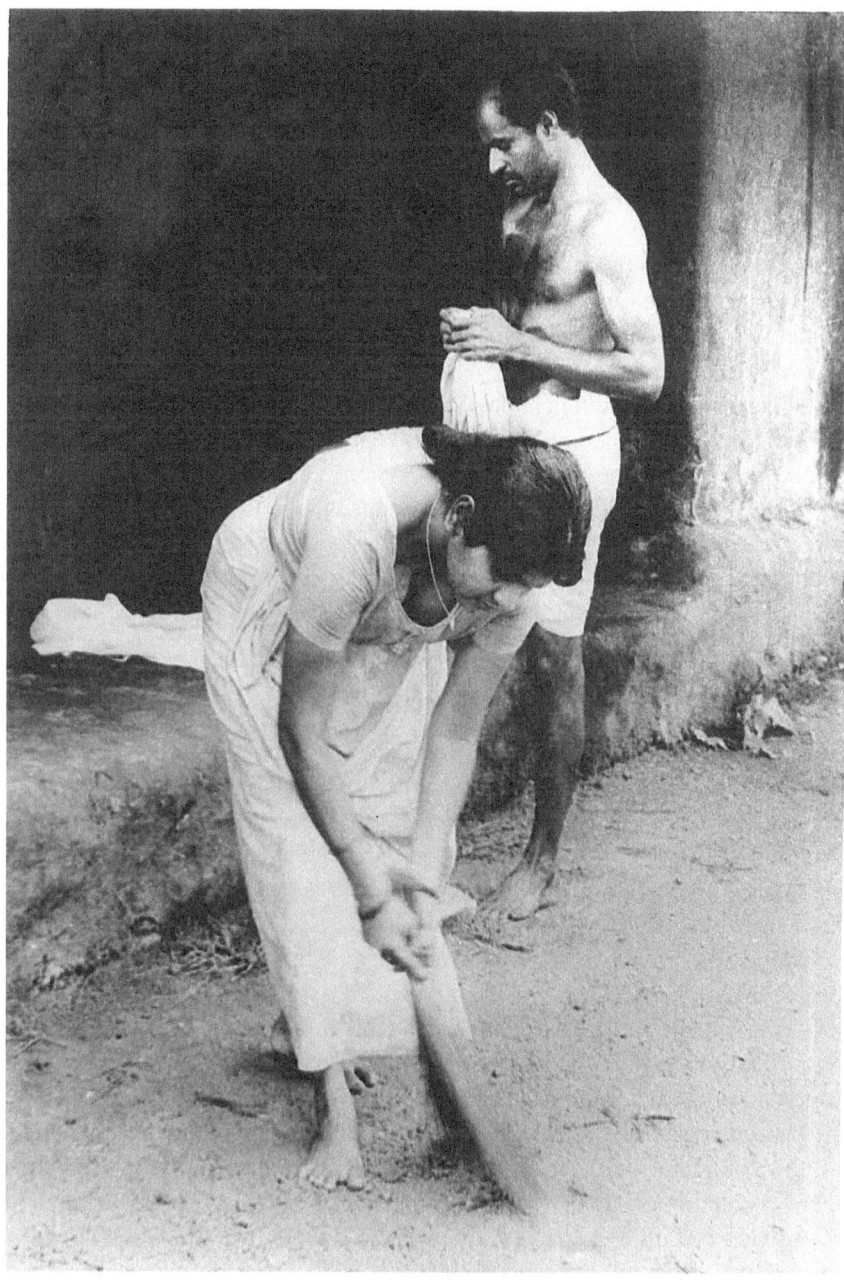

Fig. 10. *Kodiyettam*. Santhamma ignores Sankarankutty after another escapade.

According to tradition, the visiting son-in-law is fed lavishly by his in-laws, but, of course, any allusions to food in this case would be unthinkable. However, we know Santhamma is nursing her child, so there is once again a subtle allusion to food and feeding. But Sankarankutty is cut off from all forms of nurturing on this visit.

The mother-in-law's sharp jibe—"Are you a man?"—invites the question: If not a man, what is he? For most males in such a society, the question of manhood is invariably linked to fantasies of physical and sexual prowess. To be different, to be the Other, is to be weak and effete—in short, the emasculated male. This is how Sankarankutty now sees himself, and he urgently seeks to recover his lost phallus.

Sankarankutty's mother-in-law sees him as hopelessly trapped in the quotidian, an abject eating-drinking-procreating body that seeks gratification as an end in itself. For her, the issue of becoming a man is inseparable from the assumption of social and material responsibilities. In short, Sankarankutty must transform himself into a thoughtful and caring husband. He will eventually become such a man but, for the present, his profound sense of unease makes him seek out a strong father figure who could perhaps show him the way out of his deep insecurities.

Father Surrogates

The first such father in the film is the elderly Vasu, a wealthy landlord with a craving for liquor, good food and women. He stands for an older patriarchal tradition of power, virility and affluence that he displays by purchasing an elephant (thus creating a sensation in the village). He promises to take Sankarankutty under his wing and teach him to be a *mahout*. The pact is sealed with food and drink in a toddy shop, but things turn sour when the drunk Vasu proposes that Sarojini become his mistress. ("If you're that poor, leave her in my care.") Sankarankutty tries to defend his honor by ineffectually hurling an empty bottle at Vasu. He thus loses both job and father but displays a wounded pride that suggests burgeoning sensitivity.

The dissolute Vasu is an example of the failure of the elders—the fathers of the community—to create a proper code of public morality. And then there are the dregs of society like Sivan Pillai, who is perpetually drunk and has squandered his ill-gotten wealth on alcohol. Those who stay sober are prey to obsessive forms of behavior such as playing cards (adorned by fetishized images of women) all day. Close-ups of their strong, well-fed bodies and languid postures as well as crude details (a man digs into his ear with his finger) capture their uncouth physicality. They are too far gone to even conceive of a way of life that could prove redemptive.

There is a jump cut from Sankarankutty flinging his bottle to the steering wheel of a truck. The driver—a large, tough, macho man—is the new surrogate father who has hired Sankarankutty as a cleaner. Unlike the other men in the film, he does not bear the marks of their enervating rural milieu, nor does he live in a time warp. Instead, he is assertive to the point of being aggressive and relishes exercising power over others. He fits the popular Indian stereotype of the stern father who imposes his will on his children to coerce them into complete obedience. Acceptance of his authority is part of the social paradigm of dominance and submission. It could be argued that Sankarankutty yearns for such submission if it frees him from his terrible sense of emasculation. Accordingly, he plays willing son to autocratic father. The latter tells him straight off to stay away from liquor and remain alert and vigilant at all times. As compensation, he will give the good son driving lessons.

Sankarankutty finds himself suddenly thrust into a world of speed, machines and technology as they travel from the plains to the mountains in a symbolic upward journey. During this ascent, he learns not only about power, discipline, *machismo* and the abuse of women, but also about man-woman relationships in general. It makes him reflect on his own marriage and the possibility of salvaging it. This narrative of his self-growth parallels his evolution from cleaner to driver as he picks up skills and acquires knowledge that will turn him into a mature and self-reliant individual. The stops the two make on the road are also eye-openers for him. If he had initially been drawn to a phallocentric *machismo*, he will now reject it as a model, finding it utterly degrading both for the perpetrator and his victim.

When the driver visits his home, Sankarankutty watches him play both father and husband. In both roles, the man is aggressive and intimidating, abstaining from all outward displays of emotion. He makes sure his children meet his exacting standards and chides his son for not studying hard enough. Significantly, he does not sit down to eat with any of them, refusing even tea, thus staying aloof from all familial rituals. His short and rushed visit is only to fulfill an obligation.

During the driver's second stop, this time to visit Savitri, his mistress, Sankarkutty witnesses his transformation into the hard-drinking macho man who flies into a jealous rage at the slightest provocation. The man repeatedly asserts his ownership—since he provides for the woman and pays for her upkeep—with the threat of violence. During this visit, there is a small but significant allusion to food as Savitri serves Sankarankutty dried fish and rice, but the feeding ritual is perfunctory and functional. The modalities have changed, and the whole thing is bereft of any feeling. When she is about to pour Sankarkutty a drink, the driver stops her. As part of the regimen that now governs his life, Sankarkutty is denied even a drop.

The Three Visits

Gopalakrishnan creates three short scenes, each carefully nuanced and set apart from the others, during which Sankarankutty visits Santhamma. They are meant to symbolically parallel his three major escapades from home in the past.

The first meeting with Santhamma is in the absence of the mother. Sankarankutty stops briefly at her house to give her a gift. Moved to tears, she invites him in to see the child. The cradle still stands between them, but there is a cut to their hands next to each other on the wooden shaft. A cow moos at the start of the sequence and again when they are together. The old metaphor of nurturing is resurrected, but the context has changed, and there is now a sense of a shared space, both physical and emotional, that will, hopefully, lead to a mutually sustaining relationship. However, Sankarankutty is not invited to eat, so he is still excluded from the ritual. Until the emotional breach is fully healed and a larger social space can enfold the personal, there can be no entry into the symbolic.

On his second visit, Sankarankutty returns with another gift for his wife. This time the mother-in-law is at home and invites him to have tea, even a meal, but he is in a hurry and leaves quickly. Santhamma believes that if the latter had insisted, he would probably have agreed to stay and eat. The food discourse is thus reinserted into the film and becomes part of her desire to reclaim her nurturing role as provider but now within an expansive familial context. His refusal suggests his new awareness of the larger social ramifications of the ritual and that he no longer associates it solely with the rite of the body. If he wishes to enter the space she wants to create for them and their child, he too must become a provider in the true sense of the term. Only then can he let her feed him. The ritual, therefore, must be reconfigured within its new context of mutual sharing.

Gopalakrishnan now moves into the closing scene of the film. Sankarankutty is back at the house with yet another gift. It is the time of a temple festival and the mother is away. This sequence is, in many respects, visually identical to the one in which Santhamma confronted him after his first escapade. She is on the raised porch of her house while he, dimly lit, stands below. But instead of a frown, she smiles and asks, "Shall I serve you food?" She thus takes the initiative and, as wife and mother, welcomes him into her home, where there is now room for him as well. But he claims he has already eaten, which makes her protest that he never eats at their place. His reason for holding off this time is because the ritual—with all its newfound significance—can be effective only when they return to *his* house and make it *their* collective living space. The first meal together must be in this new home where they will provide for each other and for their child. For Sankarankutty, who once ran away from home, it will indeed be a true homecoming. Within this transformed familial space, he can finally become a man who is responsible for others and can take care of them. His story of emancipation, of body redeemed and reconfigured, must therefore include the reclamation of home.

The gift he offers her is a *pudava*—apparel. Giving clothes to the bride during a wedding is a sign that the bridegroom will look after her—an expectation Sankarankutty failed to fulfill. Now he affirms his role as provider. Santhamma breaks down and weeps while Gopalakrishnan cuts to fireworks going off at the festival to suggest the consummation of their new marriage.

The sense of ritual that this gift-giving establishes and through which the couple redefine their roles is complemented by the presence of the mythic, which is introduced via Kathakali. All through the sequence we hear the sound of a performance in the distance. Such a performance, drawing mostly on stories from India's epics, upholds values and morals with which the community identifies and deems timeless. The mythic is thus inseparable from the events that are depicted. Gopalakrishnan stages the couple's reunion in relation to such theater because, as he puts it, "Man, wife, and child eventually blend into the characters of the Kathakali performers performing in the village. It is a merging of roles."[3] Thus the private and the public fuse within the expanded frame Gopalakrishnan seeks to create for his narrative. By placing the couple and their child within such a mythic space, he gives them a larger social and cultural significance. He also creates a different sense of temporal duration for their story. Sankarankutty and Santhamma have successfully transformed a one-sided, self-serving rite into a complex ritual and, in the process, reconfigured their identities and affirmed a set of values that connect them to the enduring social paradigms of their community. Now, at the end of the film, their entry into the symbolic is complete.

Chapter 5

THE SEARCH FOR HOME: *SWAYAMVARAM* AND THE STRUGGLE WITH CONSCIENCE

Swayamvaram (*One's Own Choice*, 1972), Gopalakrishnan's very first feature, was an immediate sensation. It swept practically all the major national film awards in India. Hailed as a landmark in the history of Indian cinema, it self-consciously sought to assert its otherness as a new form of cinematic discourse intent on breaking all the rules. It was a call to arms against the crude, melodramatic, formulaic films of the south, especially Kerala. It bristled with innovative visual and auditory effects and boasted a complex narrative form—a mix of documentary, fiction, and fantasy—that sought to interrogate film as film. It also subscribed to an evocative poetic realism drawing on metaphor and symbol, which was unprecedented in the history of southern cinema. Many of these innovations became staples of the New Wave when it evolved into a pan-Indian phenomenon a few years later.

The story is deceptively simple. Sita and Viswanathan, both from the middle class, are runaway lovers who come to Trivandrum to live together as an unwed couple. They start out dreamy-eyed but watch their hopes flounder in their struggle to survive. On one level, the film covers well-trodden terrain about the fight to stay alive in the harsh and unforgiving environment of a small town. (Unlike most states in India, there is no rural-urban divide in Kerala, and hence no metropolitan centers. The area is best described as "rurban.") Like *Kodiyettam*, *Swayamvaram* also features a marriage, except it has no legal sanction and is based entirely on mutual trust, love and commitment, which sustain the couple as they deal with their hard lot. When Viswanathan dies from an unspecified illness, Sita, now alone with their child, must make a choice with regard to her future. The film thus begins with a choice and ends with the possibility of another one.

The couple's decision to live outside wedlock is, of course, a radical one within an orthodox society where women are taught to prize their virginity and marriages are arranged by parents, especially the all-powerful father.

Viswanathan and Sita have thus violated a major taboo, the consequences of which play out in scenarios of guilt and self-punishment. Despite the modernity of their choice (which Gopalakrishnan wholeheartedly endorses), the couple cannot handle the moral and psychological fallout from their decision. The lovers (especially Viswanathan) grapple with terrible feelings of self-doubt and remorse in what becomes a serious crisis of conscience. The emancipation that modernity promises crashes on the rocks of a profound internal crisis. Gopalakrishnan disregards the actual moment of collision between adversarial forces that led to the couple leaving home but locates the conflict in its aftermath, in an interior space.

Swayamvaram, like *Elippathayam* and *Vidheyan*, focuses on the politics of dislocation and survival (both physical and moral) in which the search for home, self and identity becomes a key issue. Like *Kodiyettam*, it is set in the 1970s but addresses—in more specific terms—the crisis of values in post-Nehruvian India. It makes multiple allusions to political rallies, chronic unemployment, inequality and injustice, and corruption and criminality, all of which have some bearing on the lives of the couple. Within such a milieu, Gopalakrishnan seeks to define a space for his protagonists, who gradually drift from the center to the margins as their economic situation deteriorates. The question is whether they can indeed wrest such a space from their semi-urban setting where competing forces vie for every available inch. As their hardships increase, they come in contact with unsavory characters who inhabit its margins. Sita, as the film's desired object, seems especially vulnerable to the sexual predators around her; there is also the terrifying possibility that one day she may have to compromise her own morals to support herself and her child. Her story would have had a different ending had it been set in rural Kerala with its sense of community and shared values, but at the end of the film, she is alone and faced with challenges that are unique to her locale. While her newfound sense of independence and selfhood links her to a progressive vision of womanhood, she is also at risk of being a casualty of a patriarchal culture that preys on women.

The theme of the outsider is, of course, obvious in *Swayamvaram*, given the premise of the film. Viswanathan and Sita are from northern Kerala, but the exact location is never revealed because they do not wish to divulge their pasts. As an unwed couple, they must hide behind the facade of a marriage or face ostracism. Accordingly, they live out a lie. Since Gopalakrishnan does not explain what prompted their flight, "home" becomes a complex psychological space, a repository of memories and emotions that are never fully defined by either one of them. It is a space to which Sita returns in her nightmares, and that produces in Viswanathan strong feelings of guilt and regret that eventually overpower him. Thus while they are materially free, they remain prisoners within their pasts. We can only surmise that their decision to flee was a fight against orthodoxy in its most destructive forms of repression and control.

Bus to Fantasy Land

When the film opens, Vishwanathan and Sita are on a bus bound for Trivandrum. This extended sequence, almost seven minutes long, is shot with very few cuts. Real time is virtually conflated with film time, and duration is a key issue. Nothing of any consequence takes place—people get on and off at regular intervals, doze, chat or do nothing as they wait out their journey. It is this sense of the impersonal and banal coupled with a strong feeling of monotony that comes to define the mood of *Swayamvaram*. Viswanathan and Sita's love story unfolds against such drab sameness while the film reiterates the routine of their daily existence.

When the camera singles out the couple, it is done in a casual, offhand way, in long shot, to suggest that they are no different from the others on the bus. In fact, the first time we see them, their backs are turned to the camera. However, in close-up, they immediately acquire their sense of individuality, taking pleasure in each other, holding hands, smiling coyly—all the signs of a young couple in love that set them apart. But their separateness remains fragile as the anonymous faces and bodies threaten to erase whatever uniqueness they possess. Meanwhile, the bus drives on with an absurd predictability in league with linear time.

Although this documentary-like prologue is not a sequence shot, the cuts are carefully cued to create a sense of uninterrupted space-time continuum. The sheer length of it, which challenges the normal span of a shot and during which there is no "action", denies viewing pleasure and subverts audience expectations. We become part of a self-referential process in which we interrogate a realism that, by its sheer insistence and duration, becomes unnatural, suspect and problematic. As we grow restive and try to figure out the point of it all, Gopalakrishnan ends the sequence with a jump cut to a traffic STOP sign, thus jolting us out of our on-screen immersion. We immediately become hyper-conscious of our relationship to the film as well as the constructed nature of reality and its representation. It seems only fitting that a film that will repeatedly draw attention to itself as film should start in a reflexive mode.

The length of the bus journey creates, among other things, a sense of the distance covered by Viswanathan and Sita. The rest of the film will show how they must negotiate a set of complex physical and mental spaces in their search for home. These journeys form a trajectory from the center to the periphery, from luxurious daydreams to rude awakenings, from the illusion of self-sufficiency to degrading impoverishment.

We first see Viswanathan and Sita occupy a room in a plush hotel in the very heart of Trivandrum, but she is often shown framed by the window, looking out, her sense of space seemingly oppressive. This feeling of confinement is probably more psychological than material while both of them seek to come to terms with the enormity of their decision. There are cutaways from her point of view to a girl reading on a terrace and to the street, and, as a procession of devotional singers passes below, the sound invades their room. The presence of larger realities existing outside is combined with a sensation of randomness and flux. The hotel, surrounded by space that seems to stretch beyond the frame, without beginning or end, offers no sense of a stable center. Gopalakrishnan inserts a fairly long fantasy sequence at this juncture to foreground their need for escape but refuses to identify it with any particular point of view. It remains enigmatic, its authorship uncertain, its intentions never fully articulated. It is replete with over-the-top histrionics of the sort one encounters in commercial films, but it also contains serious undertones that only become clear later in the film.

From a stylized shot of Sita reaching out to Viswanathan as he lies in bed with his arms open to embrace her—a prelude to their lovemaking—there is a cut to her all dolled up as a movie star, running on the seashore towards the camera until she is almost out of focus. Viswanathan joins her, also made up garishly, and they play out a movie romance, striking a whole gamut of stereotyped postures while the sea breaks around them. Their performance in this film-within-a-film is apparently fueled by the reveries and daydreams of mainstream cinema that, for the middle class, often constitute the real thing. As they indulge in a honeymoon fantasy, the scenes feature shaky hand-held shots, jump cuts, dramatic zooms and close-ups, all accompanied by a high-decibel music soundtrack. We witness a parody of the kind of cinema Gopalakrishnan rejects unequivocally. By creating the abrupt collision of two divergent visual styles—one based on poetic realism and documentary, the other drawing on melodrama—he defines his own place and credo as a filmmaker.

The fantasy insert includes three episodes, each shot in the same campy style. As Viswanathan clambers down some slippery rocks towards the sea, Sita, in long shot, beckons to him from above, warning him of the dangers of losing his foothold. But Viswanathan, the show-off, carries on all the way down. In the second episode, she finds him head down on the train tracks and manages to pull him away just as the train arrives. As they embrace, there is a cut to a movie poster of a couple embracing, followed by more shots of such poster lovers, ending with Viswanathan and Sita wrapped in a bear hug. Finally, we see Sita running through a set of diverse landscapes, each time in a different *sari*, looking desperately for Viswanathan, when suddenly a hand is thrust into the frame and grabs her. With this sudden intrusion of reality—the threat of abduction and rape—the daydream-turned-nightmare ends abruptly. In the next shot, we see the lovers sitting pensively on the beach.

All viewers of popular Indian cinema would immediately identify with these clichéd stock situations and overblown emotions. While Viswanathan gets away with his cheap stunts, it is Sita, the woman, who is reduced to making oversized, hysterical gestures. In the third and most ambiguous episode, she is allowed to become the protagonist only because Viswanathan has disappeared, leaving her alone and abandoned. We sense her hysteria as she looks around wildly before breaking into a run. When the hand reaches out for her, it signals, at first, the sort of crude, melodramatic rape scenario that is often the staple of mainstream cinema. Only later in the film do we realize that the scene relates to a dream during which her father gave her chase. The three episodes, then, also allude to the couple's deep-rooted insecurities and are more complex than they seem at first. In retrospect, the train track sequence is an ominous portent of Viswanathan's death. In fact, all three segments directly or indirectly allude to his eventual disappearance from Sita's life. Thus the main features of their story—romance, loss and Sita's possible sexual enslavement—are filtered through kitsch to set up a contrast with the harsh realities they will soon face. As the film chronicles the hardships they endure, we see no resemblance whatsoever to their movie surrogates. Viswanathan comes across as brooding and pensive, Sita thoughtful and serious. She cares deeply for him but never turns to melodrama to express her feelings. Nor is she ever portrayed as the helpless woman, utterly dependent on him. The fantasy, in this respect, is a parodic rendition of the couple's dalliance with the world of make-believe— just before they get down to the serious business of living.

The Precariousness of Space

Given their limited resources, Viswanathan and Sita have to abandon their new "home"—the upscale hotel—shortly after they check in. It is the first of many wake-up calls in the film. The second hotel is predictably cheaper but also drab and squalid, offering little privacy. In their room, Sita discovers soiled bed sheets and empty liquor bottles under the bed. The room thus bears traces of its previous occupancy that impinge on the present and, as the couple discovers, tie them to people they have never met. The film subsequently develops this idea of how spaces vacated by their previous occupants preserve histories and memories that affect those who enter and inhabit them. Sita, as a woman, is affected the most. We see this happen, in fact, right after they shift in. When Viswanathan is out one day, a stranger knocks on their door. When she opens it, the man tries to force his way in. Accustomed to soliciting questionable favors from the previous resident, he mistakes her for the absent person. He comes to exemplify a faceless sexual threat that could be all too real one day. In fact, as Viswanathan and Sita are forced to compromise their access to space because of money, the issue of morality is repeatedly foregrounded since, with every move, there is a corresponding decline in the moral climate around them. The issue of staying "clean" becomes pivotal.

During their stay in this second temporary home, away from the center of the town, Viswanathan and Sita witness the eviction of a tenant who claims his money was stolen from his room—apparently a ruse to avoid paying his dues. He is physically manhandled and ejected by the staff. The scene is revealing in the way it focuses on the same specter of eviction that hangs over Viswanathan and Sita. Also, the tenant's moral chicanery coupled with the hotel owner's use of force paint a dismal picture of urban life where no place is safe and human integrity is always suspect.

Their next move takes Viswanathan and Sita to a house on the town's outskirts that is essentially a hovel consisting of a room, kitchen and porch. Inside is the same story of filth and disorder, but this time, there are live occupants: white ants who have built a nest on the door, a cockroach that scampers across a calendar on the wall and a centipede that Sita picks up with her broom and throws out. These auguries are not good. The bare rooms, bereft of human presence and taken over by denizens of another world, are a denial of everything that resembles a home, especially for a couple who have suffered two recent displacements. The sordid history of the place only compounds their sense of alienation. They learn that the previous tenant was a corrupt clerk who accepted bribes, thus tarnishing the "memory" of the house. But Viswanathan and Sita manage—undeterred—to carve out a domestic space that they hope will absorb and enfold their otherness as strangers. It will be a precarious existence, living right on the edge, their feelings for each other their only source of strength and hope. Although they will not have to move again, the threat of eviction remains as Viswanathan struggles to find a job. Thus for a couple we first met on a moving bus, this new home predictably lacks strong foundations and remains a transitory, fragile space at best.

Viswanathan and Sita soon discover that their new life in the margins has placed them in close proximity to people who not only belong to the lower rungs of society but who, morally and materially, are outsiders in relation to mainstream social and cultural practices—a point of affinity that is not lost on the unwed couple. Some live profoundly impoverished lives while others grab every opportunity to make illicit money. What separates Viswanathan and Sita from the latter is not only their class and education but the fact of their personal integrity, which has given them the courage to live outside wedlock. However, what bonds them all together is the critical battle for survival in the face of which social divisions crumble. Viswanathan and Sita know only too well that if their economic crisis deepens, they could very well end up with those around them inhabiting their space, living their life.

The Leveling of Differences

The leveling of differences as a concept is broached on a number of occasions in the film, generally within the context of mistaken identity. For example, Sita receives a letter addressed to the former tenant of the house. The next time the mistake is more serious, made by a policeman who bangs on her door in the middle of the night while Viswanathan is away (an obvious reference to the earlier knocking on the hotel door) (Figure 11). He assumes she is Kalyani, the prostitute who lives next door. Sita thus finds herself identified with a disreputable woman. Earlier, three drunks had brazenly knocked on their door at night. When Viswanathan had confronted them, they confused him with the previous resident, asking him about his shady dealings and how he got hold of such a beautiful woman. As with Sita's misplaced identity, Viswanathan finds himself being treated as a drinking buddy, an old friend of three depraved men. Even in mistaken circumstances, the possibility of Viswanathan and Sita merging with the dregs of society is a real one.

Fig. 11. *Swayamvaram*. Sita mistaken for Kalyani by a policeman.

Of her immediate neighbors, there are two women Sita befriends. Janaki, a widow, sells rice to make a living; she is warm-hearted, caring and genuinely concerned about Sita's welfare. Kalyani, who is from the working class and whose alcoholic husband is mostly absent, embodies the decadent life. Her favored client is the corrupt Vasu, a smuggler by profession, who casts a lecherous eye on Sita. He is, in a sense, the ultimate predator in relation to all the men who desire her. When he first covets her with his gaze, Kalyani warns him that it is an impossible dream, but he is sure he will net his prey. Shortly after this scene, Sita has a terrible nightmare and, a little later, Viswanathan loses his job. As if on cue, the three drunks appear as an evil portent of things to come. Vasu's evil eye seems to have set a whole slew of events in motion.

There is also a scene in which Vasu subtly offers to buy Sita. So far he has ogled her from the lane and from Kalyani's window without daring to pay the couple a visit. One night, he shows up on their porch with the pretext of paying a social call. As he makes small talk with Viswanathan (Sita stays in her room), he offers him an illegally procured foreign watch. The insinuation is that Viswanathan can pay for it with his wife. No such deal is struck, but spatially Vasu has moved much closer to the couple.

Gopalakrishnan repeatedly sets up correspondences—both direct and implied—between the two couples: Viswanathan and Sita, and Vasu and Kalyani. Because they have virtually nothing in common, this may seem puzzling until we realize that both couples are guilty of having flouted certain social and moral codes.

Although Vasu does not live with Kalyani, he spends a great deal of his time in her room. In fact, their scenes together suggest a marriage of sorts that sets up a parallel with Viswanathan and Sita's own "marriage." There is, however, an obvious, crucial difference. Vasu's relationship with Kalyani revolves around lucre and the pleasures of the flesh, which is a violation of public morality. The unwed couple next door is also guilty of a moral and social indiscretion, but money doesn't govern their commitment to each other, which they regard as stronger than anything else, including a legally sanctioned marriage. And yet Gopalakrishnan suggests larger affinities between the couples that are literal as well as metaphorical in nature. For example, we see Vasu waking up in Kalyani's bed. When he asks for tea, she obliges. Later, on another occasion, Kalyani buttons his shirt. Both actions will be duplicated by the other couple but not in the same circumstances.

Physically there is no resemblance between Kalyani and Sita. They have different physiognomies and wear different clothes as well. Kalyani, in keeping with her working class background, dresses in a blouse and *mundu*, while the middle class Sita is always in a *sari*. However, after Viswanathan dies, Sita is associated with clothes that are identical to those worn by her neighbor. This is a critical period in her life when she must—without any material resources of her own—determine her future. Will she take the same route as Kalyani? The question is never answered, but the possibility is hinted at through the associations Gopalakrishnan creates.

Earlier in the film, we see an image (probably from a calendar) of a woman on Kalyani's bedroom wall that vaguely resembles the gaudily dressed Sita of the fantasy insert, except that it has a more sexualized look, probably for the benefit of the men who visit her. The insinuation here is that Sita, too, like her neighbor, could become an object of desire, looked at and solicited by men, and it would be entirely due to her own conscious choice. Within her home, she is associated with the image of a goddess on her wall; the juxtaposition of the sacred and the profane helps us define Sita's dilemma at the end of the film, when she must choose whether to compromise her morals or not.

A similar allusion to her future is made by juxtaposing two scenes. When Kalyani's wastrel husband visits her and pleads for his liquor money, Viswanathan witnesses the scene from the porch of his house. When the man leaves, there is a cut to the interior of Kalyani's room, where a client sits on her bed. Clearly, this arrangement meets with the tacit approval of the spouse. Later in the film, Sita is also associated with the porch, as she takes Viswanathan's place and watches bemusedly as Kalyani refuses money to her husband. What we see is a travesty of the relationship that Viswanathan and Sita enjoy, which is based on mutual caring, trust and self-respect; there is nothing remotely sordid about their life together. And yet, as their financial situation rapidly deteriorates, we wonder how long it would take for things to change. Would Sita end up with a client in her room (who could very well be Vasu)? Would Viswanathan look the other way? Would he become dependent on Sita's earnings? It also begs the question whether Kalyani is Sita's repressed alter ego. By asking us to link the two scenes, Gopalakrishnan opens up multiple possible readings.

Sita's Sense of Her Impurity

One of the questions the film poses is whether Sita herself subconsciously identifies with Kalyani, seeing a shadow of her own future in the prostitute. This identification may run even deeper if she regards herself as impure and tainted for sleeping with a man who is not legally her husband. In fact, there is enough evidence in the film to suggest that this may indeed be the case.

Despite the strong front Sita puts up in public, her double life causes her profound unease. To keep up the pretense of marriage, she even wears a *thali*, which is associated with married women. Taught to believe in the sanctity of marriage as well as the purity of a woman's body prior to wedlock,

Sita's repressed guilt surfaces in her nightmares. The lie of playing Viswanathan's wife conflicts with the traditional middle class values that she has internalized more than she realizes.

In one such nightmare, she sees herself standing in a lotus-filled temple pond. As she reaches down to pluck them, she starts to sink, pulled down by invisible hands that belong to her father. When she calls out to Viswanathan for help, he is nowhere to be found. In the final segment of the dream, her father chases her through a forest. Since the temple pond carries connotations of the sacred, her paralyzing fear, at first, seems to apply to her inherent sense of impurity (the dream occurs shortly after she discovers she is pregnant). But there is also the dread of being apprehended and punished by her father for her profane acts—defiance of his authority, defilement of her body and violation of her morals. That she was about to pluck lotuses is significant because it alludes to her deep-rooted anxiety about losing her virginity—a terrifying sin in a society in which unmarried women must safeguard their chastity. A Western reading would impute a rape or abuse scenario featuring the father, but that does not seem to be Gopalakrishnan's intent. While sexual violation is certainly an issue here, it has its source in Sita's own sense of having compromised her body and brought shame on herself, her father and her family. To be pulled down into the water is also to drown—a death that Sita knows women often seek in such circumstances and that her father may even secretly wish for.

In the dream's last section, the specter of retribution still hangs heavy over Sita as she finds herself relentlessly pursued by the man. Viswanathan's absence, his inability to come to her rescue, implies abandonment, which not only points to his eventual death but perhaps also to his failure to provide her with the material security she longs for. Thus her sense of being alone, let down by both father and lover and having to fend for herself is central to the dream.

There are some correspondences between Sita's nightmare and the earlier fantasy insert in which we witnessed instances of Viswanathan's daredevilry followed by shots of her running through a forest, looking desperately for him (the same soundtrack featuring animal and bird cries is used for both scenes). The scene ended with her possible abduction or rape. Viswanathan's death is obviously presaged by his courting danger on the rocks or placing his head on the train tracks. Although none of this surfaces in the dream, his very absence is telling. The threat of sexual violation that is broached in both sequences could—as we saw—stem from Sita's strong feelings of guilt. But in the fantasy insert, it acquires a sense of imminence that is deeply disturbing. Does it allude to a future without Viswanathan when Sita could face rape or, as a bedfellow of her clients, succumb to institutionalized rape?

Gopalakrishnan wants us to place both sequences within the contexts in which he has vividly defined a sordid sexuality: the soiled bedsheets and empty liquor bottles; the predatory glances Sita must bear; the stranger knocking on the door; the advent of the three drunks; Sita being mistaken for Kalyani; and, of course, the lecherous gaze of the dissolute Vasu. Although he does not ever question the integrity of Sita's choice to live with Viswanathan, he suggests that it is not simply a matter of chance that she encounters disreputable men and women or finds herself in dubious situations. The truth is that she is subconsciously and inexorably drawn to them from her own sense of guilt and insecurity. She gravitates, as it were, to those who have openly and consciously embraced the "other" life, as she believes she has herself, and thus identifies with prostitutes like Kalyani.

Sita as Nurturing Goddess

The troubling image of Sita as the victim of circumstances beyond her control is balanced by her more positive representation as a self-sacrificing, caring woman like Rajamma or Saroja. She repeatedly offers emotional succor to her guilt-wracked husband, and her relationship to Sukumaran—the neighbor's young son—is replete with maternal feelings. She is also associated with food, cooking and serving, making her a wholesome provider in the true sense of the term. In these respects, she surpasses the other women, acquiring the nurturing qualities of a Hindu goddess and thus taking on a mythic persona. But, at the same time, she is not a mere nurturer and does not allow her life to be circumscribed by such a role. In fact, there are multiple Sitas in the film. On one occasion, we see her sitting on the porch, engrossed in reading a book, happy to indulge in a simple pleasure within her own space. We also see her hunting for a job to supplement Viswanathan's meager income, becoming his partner and equal in the process. Sita consistently displays an independent mind and a certain resourcefulness that sustain her and Viswanathan in their ongoing battle for survival.

Gopalakrishnan expands the mythic framework, implicit in the goddess analogy, by calling her Sita, an allusion to the female protagonist of India's major epic, the *Ramayana*. The title of the film also refers to the epic, since Sita chose Rama, her husband, at her *swayamvara*—a gathering in ancient India where a woman chose a husband from her assembled suitors. The calendar in Sita's room depicts her namesake at such an event.

For most Indians, Sita embodies the ideal of Indian womanhood: virtuous and pure in heart and mind, faithful and devoted to Rama, her husband. Even her abduction and confinement by Ravana, the demon king, could not tarnish her reputation or compromise her morals. We are asked to apply this image of chasteness to Sita in the film because she too manages to defeat the Ravanas who threaten her. However, the fact that she lives in sin and has a child out of wedlock complicates the whole ethical issue. But, for Gopalakrishnan, it is a non-issue because he does not doubt the innate purity of her intentions or the strength of her convictions. Her commitment to Viswanathan and the choice they have made redeem her from society's attempt to brand her as a fallen woman. He thus reformulates the Sita myth and offers a radically different definition of purity outside its prescribed meanings.

In the *Ramayana*, Sita has to undergo a purification ritual by stepping into fire to prove that she was not defiled during her incarceration by Ravana; she passes the test successfully. Gopalakrishnan implies that Sita, by virtue of her integrity, can also pass the test.

Since in Sanskrit, *swayam* means self and *vara* means choice or desire, the English title of the film—*One's Own Choice*—also invokes the choices Sita must make as a woman and individual. This is given a mythic framework as well because her neighbors Kalyani and Janaki bear names that also apply to Sita in the epic. The two women in the film embody diametrically opposite lifestyles, modes of survival and ethical points of view, Kalyani being the whore and Janaki the caring neighbor. It is evident in the film's double ending that they symbolize the two paths Sita faces after Viswanathan dies. Will she remain chaste and stainless like her mythical namesake or plunge into the sordid life of a prostitute?

In the film's last section, widowed and grieving, Sita seems to be in a daze, living within and yet outside linear time (Figure 12). A series of fade-outs and fade-ins convey her liminal state. Janaki urges her to return to her parents, while Viswanathan's friend and coworker, Kanakka Pillai, invites her to live with him and his family. Sita says no to both. When she left her parents, she stopped being a daughter; now Viswanathan's death frees her from being a "wife." Sita seems content to be just a woman and mother and embraces her independence. But the question of her survival and that of her child remains unresolved and deeply problematic. Gopalakrishnan associates her repeatedly with the boy whose joyful presence implies the renewal of life but also points to a future full of uncertainty.

The film's final sequence quite eloquently describes Sita's state of mind. While she cools milk for the baby, we hear the singing voices from the fantasy insert. It provides a sobering moment of reflection as we recall the exuberance of the star-struck lovers on the beach. As Sita feeds the child, flashes of lightning illuminate the calendar image of Sita on the wall, recalling her mythic persona. Shots of the locked door alternate with shots of the child sleeping and of Sita glancing off-screen toward the door. Finally, the camera stays on her face, and the shot changes to a freeze, followed by a slow fade-out.

Fig. 12. *Swayamvaram*. Sita after Viswanathan's death.

The film thus leaves Sita poised on the threshold of change. The door serves both as a marker of new beginnings as well as a reminder of the dissolute men who have knocked on it. Alone and without resources, she seems especially vulnerable to falling prey to such men. But the look on her face belies such a reading. At the hour of crisis, faced with a future bereft of prospects, she does not appear confused or fearful but calm and composed. The freeze leaves her suspended in time and gives her a space within which she can make her life-transforming decision. She is simply Sita in this final shot, not belonging to anyone, but a woman who must find the strength to forge a new life and a new self for her sake and that of her child.

Viswanathan's Dark Night of the Soul

Sita struggles with her repressed guilt in her nightmares, but Viswanathan's guilt assumes the proportions of a malady that eventually consumes him. His very first words in the film are "Did we do wrong?" This feeling of having violated some immutable moral law will be compounded by his sense of having failed Sita as man and "husband" because he is unable to provide her with a strong economic foundation. His inner sickness eventually translates into a death wish—the ultimate punishment he seeks for his transgressions and inadequacies. Like Sita, but to a much larger extent, he struggles unsuccessfully with the ethical ramifications of the choice he has made.

Viswanathan stands out as a man who is essentially decent and goodhearted, free from the usual vices and the destructive addictions to drink, food and women we encounter in many of Gopalakrishnan's males. Mild-mannered and sensitive, he has creative aspirations and yearns for literary success. His only shortcoming is perhaps a certain naiveté that makes him a dreamer and an idealist, not quite ready to handle the harsh realities of their new life. During the course of the film, we see his brutal initiation and the shattering of his illusions. His dream of getting published comes to nothing when his novel is rejected for serialization by a literary journal. The tutorial college that hires him goes bankrupt and cancels his contract. Eventually he gets a job as clerk in a sawmill factory, but his meager salary can barely sustain him and Sita.

In the aftermath of his defeats, Gopalakrishnan generally shows Viswanathan in bed, utterly dejected, while Sita carries out her daily household chores. A revealing contrast is set up between his inertness and her busy, purposeful movements. He remains cut off from the dynamic space she creates, consumed by apathy and inaction as well as guilt because he cannot rouse himself to help her. On one occasion he calls out to her, but it is only to confront her with the same question (always the same question): "Did we do wrong?" He has an almost childlike need for comfort and reassurance that she, as the nurturing woman, immediately provides. In his abject state, he believes his woes are indeed a form of retribution for his sins. Gopalakrishnan even shoots from a high angle as if to suggest some sort of wrathful nemesis hovering over the depressed man. Despite Sita's efforts to bolster his spirits, Viswanathan cannot extricate himself from this feeling of gloom and doom. The emotional succor she offers him only deepens his helplessness and sense of disempowerment.

Twice, Viswanathan is associated with left-wing political rallies. These boisterous all-male gatherings offer him same-sex solidarity as well as a common ideological platform. Both rallies express anger and outrage at the injustices inflicted on the common man, a subject that is deeply pertinent to Viswanathan. The first time, he actually joins the crowd and listens to the speaker denounce all political parties as bourgeois, with their sole aim to mislead and manipulate the workers. He listens passively, more, it seems, out of curiosity than any real desire to participate in the rally. Since he is jobless and deeply insecure, his apparent lack of enthusiasm is puzzling. Soon he loses interest and wanders off, only to run into a prostitute who solicits him from the shadows. He ignores her.

The second time, the rally is far in the distance. We see Viswanathan walk down a lane, moving from medium to long shot in a single long take while the cries of the protesters can be heard. As the camera holds onto him, there is again a sense of his detachment, his physical and ideological separation from the political war being waged at the end of what seems an interminably long side street. Because he has recently lost his job at the tutorial, one would imagine that Viswanathan would strongly identify with a crowd whose slogan is "Reinstate retrenched workers," but he watches the rally go by as the cries of the protesters grow faint. This time, it is an impoverished man drinking from a faucet who connects with his gaze as he walks away.

Both sequences suggest that Viswanathan is either disillusioned with organized political action (much of the rhetoric at the first rally is predictably clichéd) or simply too self-absorbed and apathetic. He seems incapable of seeing his problems as part of a larger pattern that can be addressed only through collective intervention. This is implied when he comes face to face with the two symbols of the disenfranchised masses. The prostitute and the man at the faucet are far worse off than he is, but their gazes suggest that he and they are part of a common cause, partners in the same battle for survival. But Viswanathan may not be willing to acknowledge this possibility as of yet. The fact that the voices from the rally are far-off and ineffectual adds a layer of irony. Later in the film, Viswanathan encounters a hand-cart puller completely weighed down by a load of logs that he is transporting uphill to the sawmill factory. It is an almost archetypal image of the oppressed, toiling man in an unequal world. Although glances are not exchanged, the message to the sawmill clerk is to let go of his aloof superiority and see himself as one of them.

Viswanathan initially tries to ignore these signs, but soon finds himself locked into a situation from which there is no apparent escape. He is accosted one day on the street by a man who worked for the same sawmill factory for 12 years before being unjustly fired. In fact, it turns out that he held the very job that Viswanathan has been given. The angry man asks him not to be a party to such unethical action. As Viswanathan walks away, he's told not to behave like "a white-collared big shot."

The most ethically and politically correct action would be to resign and agitate on behalf of the retrenched worker (as the rally urged with one voice), but such idealism is a luxury that Viswanathan can ill afford. He can empathize with the man's dire economic situation and the injustice done to him but is powerless to act on the man's behalf. Thus Viswanathan's dilemma boils down to this: he cannot let go of his job because his survival depends on it, and, at the same time, he cannot get the man off his conscience. By linking the political rally's slogan to Viswanathan's personal crisis, Gopalakrishnan reminds us of his inability to relate his private woes to the complex historical and political processes unfolding around him.

As the laid-off worker begins to confront Viswanathan daily, he becomes the symbol of a nameless dread to be feared and avoided. There are shots of Viswanathan looking up from his desk to the window where the man stands with his relentless, unflinching, accusing gaze. Gradually, the worker becomes a physical projection of the larger guilt that has been devouring Viswanathan since he eloped with Sita. Like her, he invariably finds himself in situations that allude to his internal conflicts. It is almost as if he wills these encounters as he struggles with his conscience. If he has an unconscious desire to be punished, it takes the form of his final illness—an externalization of his inner sickness.

As Viswanathan lies inert and gravely ill, his approaching death is played out in the contexts of renewal and the resurgence of life via an expressive soundtrack and the strong presence of the child whose crying grows louder and louder, as if in anticipation of his father's loss. Such an ending may seem clichéd, but Gopalakrishnan manages to infuse genuine feeling into the scene. Viswanathan dies an agonizing death from his self-inflicted internal wounds, but such a tragic end to human potential is countered by new life and hope, as is often the case in Gopalakrishnan's cinema.

However uplifting such a vision may be, *Swayamvaram* is essentially about failure. This theme applies not only to Viswanathan and Sita but to the community at large, which seems incapable—in the context of the '70s—of pulling itself together in the face of demoralization and defeat. Somewhat like the villagers in *Mukhamukham*, the people can neither organize themselves nor come up with an agenda for change. Prey to self-doubt and uncertainty, they fail to act decisively in order to bring about their own political and social transformation, hence the presence of the prostitute, the beggar, the man dragging an inhuman load, the drunks and the corrupt smuggler.

With regard to Viswanathan and Sita, although they take the extraordinary and crucial step of breaking free from the stranglehold of orthodoxy, they cannot fully accept the consequences of their choice. The codes they have rejected reassert themselves as the couple is assailed by guilt. Neither can transcend their feelings of wrongdoing, remorse and regret, so much so that Viswanathan, as we see, succumbs to the ultimate self-punishment—death. Thus while the film upholds the modernity of their choice and bid for freedom, the couple eventually fail to live up to the expectations generated by that choice. The regressive forces win at the end, but Sita, despite her debilitating self-image, emerges stronger and more resilient. In the final frames of the film, she is poised to determine her future on her own terms, and her decision will change her life forever. She has thus grown through her experiences in a way that was not possible for the weak and vacillating Viswanathan. In fact, she has evolved significantly from where she was at the start of *Swayamvaram*. However tentative, this constitutes a sign of hope at the end of the film.

Chapter 6

WOMAN IN THE DOORWAY: *NAALU PENNUNGAL* AND *ORU PENNUM RANDAANUM*

There are primarily two dominant tropes associated with women in Gopalakrishnan's cinema. One, as we've seen, is food and feeding, which is linked to nurturing and the role of the provider. The other is the doorway against which women are often framed. Both tropes are, of course, not mutually exclusive and often appear in conjunction with one another in the same film. We've already encountered strong nurturing women like Sita, Santhamma, Rajamma and Saroja, who are also identified with the doorway. And then there is the tragic Omana, whose life seems to revolve around it. In Gopalakrishnan's most recent films, *Naalu Pennungal* (*Four Women*, 2007) and *Oru Pennum Randaanum* (*A Climate for Crime*, 2008), it is the doorway that tends to assert itself both literally and metaphorically (when it is not invoked visually). This is especially true for the first film, in which women seek voice and visibility within a society that often seeks to silence and marginalize them. The doorway embodies their sense of insecurity, exclusion and otherness.

Although Kerala has had a long history of matrilineal communities run by women, Gopalakrishnan's films are mostly concerned with the aftermath, when such communities have declined and men have gained ascendancy. The woman in the doorway exemplifies this change in status. Standing on the edge of what is often the public space within the house, she is at best a witness to what men discuss and decide. Social convention has taught her to be circumspect in their presence, for it would be deemed unseemly to step forward and join them in their deliberations. Thus she stands, listens and observes. The men, in turn, acknowledge her presence, but always with a certain ambivalence: she is visible and yet invisible, present and yet absent.

Her domain is the space behind and around her—the domestic sphere of kitchen and bedroom—where she is granted a large measure of autonomy as long as it does not conflict with the agendas set by the men. Standing in the doorway, she inhabits the borderland between these two spaces, defined by and within her liminality. At the same time, the very notion of doorway (and its implied threshold) also signifies immense possibilities that herald liberty and emancipation and acquire larger existential connotations outside the context of gender. It makes the trope dynamic and infuses it with a certain optimism. Are these women then capable of overcoming their confining, limited spaces? Can they free themselves from their marginality and redefine their senses of self? Can they achieve some form of personal transcendence?

These questions are integral to both *Naalu Pennungal* and *Oru Pennum Randaanum*, which are conceived as quartets and based on short stories by Kerala's celebrated writer Thakhazi Sivasankara Pillai. The stories in *Naalu Pennungal*, which extend from the mid-1940s to the mid-1960s, place women mostly in relation to marriage. *Oru Pennum Randaanum*, which is set in the 1940s in the princely state of Travancore, a constituent of modern-day Kerala, makes transgression—criminal, moral and social—its subject. With the exception of one story, *Niyamvum Neethiyum* (*The Police*), they all foreground women in different contexts.

Oru Niyamalanghanathinte Katha (*The Prostitute*): **The Question of Legitimacy**

In *Oru Niyamalanghanathinte Katha*, which opens *Naalu Pennungal*, Kunju Pennu, the local whore, has given up her profession in favor of a new life. Identified always as the sexual Other, she seeks to shake off her past and assume a new (and clean) identity. But the precariousness of her social status and the space she occupies is defined via the sidewalk where she sleeps every night with her partner, Pappukkutty. Her existence on the very edge of society thus acquires a certain concreteness, the sidewalk a marker of her homelessness and liminality. She needs to get off it and build a home with the man she loves. In short, she needs to move forward across the threshold of her marginality through the imaginary doorway in which she has been stuck.

Much of the film shows her efforts to carve herself a new social space by working legitimately as a laborer. As she tells her friend, even though she has to carry heavy loads of gravel on her head every day and is poorly paid, she prefers such grueling work. It sets her free from the stigma of her past and gives her a chance to remake her life. Pappukkutty, who is also a laborer, echoes her sentiments. Both endorse the work ethic and dream of leaving the street behind. In keeping with their newfound but fragile sense of self-empowerment, they declare themselves husband and wife. Their "marriage," as in *Swayamvaram*, acquires a legitimacy based on their personal commitment to each other.

In the film's first half, there are several shots of people hard at work as they build a road out in the country. Kunju Pennu, one of the few women who have been hired, keeps up with the men and tells them how much she enjoys working for a living. She is also socially at ease in their company, sitting in their midst, sipping tea like one of them. Spatially, she is no longer the woman in the margins who is sought out by men for their pleasure, but their equal. When the overseer (who probably knows about her past) makes a pass at her, she is quick to put him down, reminding him that she now lives with her man. He backs off. Kunju Pennu has always been good at speaking up, but she now draws on her new sense of legitimacy as a "married" woman to assert herself.

However, as Kunju Pennu finds out when she is back in town, it is not easy to get rid of one's past. She is still treated as the "slut queen" by most men, and when she repulses a drunk who blocks her way, he angrily retorts: Who does she think she is—a virgin? When Pappukkutty beats him up, the man brings the police to the sidewalk, where the couple is arrested for public indecency. The second half of the story is set in a court of law, where Pappukkutty and Kunju Pennu's defense, based on their claim of marriage, is shot down precisely because it lacks legitimacy. Their private vows have no relevance here, although they repeatedly affirm that they are husband and wife. They are also unable to furnish a residential address or their fathers' names, thus completely eroding their credibility. Promptly cast as "lowly folk" with dubious morals, they are sentenced to fifteen days in jail. Thus Kunju Pennu's attempt to reclaim herself socially and otherwise ends prematurely. She realizes that legitimacy, as a concept, has both private and public meanings, and the two can never converge. She also discovers that in an unforgiving, prejudicial society, as long as she occupies the sidewalk, her reputation will be at stake. Having failed to prove herself to be wife in the eyes of law, she must now fight society's attempt to brand her as a whore in perpetuity. Her dream of building a home and forging a new identity—in short, her dream of emancipation—is nipped in the bud.

Kanyaka (*The Virgin*): Not Man and Wife

This second story comes right after *Oru Niyamalanghanathinte Katha* because it, too, examines the question of legitimacy, though it does so from a very different point of view. This time it will be the wife who will deny the very basis of her marriage.

Kumari is in her late twenties and single. A strong and independent woman, she works as a farmhand to support her mother and ailing father. The film opens with the father's praise for his daughter's simple and frugal ways and her single-minded, selfless devotion to the family. The fact that she is still unmarried is, of course, a major source of concern, but the father is certain that Kumari will bring prosperity to her future home. When a go-between arranges a match, the man turns out to be an only child like her; he owns a shop and lives with his mother. Previous attempts to get him married off have failed because of his fastidiousness and his general reluctance to settle down.

When the prospective bridegroom comes to visit the family, Kumari feels shy and hangs back. Before he leaves, her female relatives arrange an impromptu meeting between them, urging her to articulate her preference. Times have changed, they remind her, and it is important to speak one's mind. But before the demure Kumari can even look him in the eye, her mother intervenes and decides for her. "She likes him," she claims peremptorily, and the matter is settled there and then. Kumari finds herself thrust into a marriage with a man she has barely set eyes on.

Gopalakrishnan's purpose here is not to turn the film into a simple critique of parental authority or the vicissitudes of arranged marriages. The mother has her reasons for intruding—she has waited long enough for Kumari to get married and sees this as her daughter's last chance to find a husband, so she takes matters into her own hand. The abrupt nature of her intervention only brings out her quiet desperation.

After the wedding, Kumari discovers that her husband is by nature reclusive and withdrawn. His overly serious demeanor—he barely smiles at all—confirms his strangeness. His mother takes pride in having brought him up strictly, and we learn from her that he neither smokes nor drinks and rarely spends any money on himself. His only indulgence is the movies—he has to watch every film on the day of its release. Kumari discovers this on her very first conjugal night, when she loses out to her husband's celluloid passion; he returns home late from the theater only to go out again on the pretext of taking a bath. Kumari sits up for him and falls asleep, her back against the wall. He never shows up. It is an ominous prelude to their marital life.

What the mother does not reveal is her son's gluttony, which provides Gopalakrishnan with yet another opportunity to introduce his favorite trope of eating. During their first post-marriage visit to Kumari's parents, the silent and passive husband comes alive when he is served food. He sets to work with the same gusto Sankarankutty displayed in *Kodiyettam*. He disregards the concerned glances of his wife and father-in-law and gorges himself at each meal. As in the earlier film, such obsessive eating contains a hidden erotic element. In the case of Kumari's husband, it is a virtually orgiastic sublimation of his repressed sexual desire. This becomes clear when we discover that their marriage neither has been nor will be consummated.

Although Gopalakrishnan does not provide an explanation for the man's sexual apathy, he points to a possible Oedipal scenario, given his father's absence and the close ties that exist between mother and son. However, a stronger case could be made for the husband's extreme self-absorption, which makes him turn away from all that which is extraneous to his life—wife and sex included.

He reminds us again of Sankarankutty, who could not accept the prospect of having to share his space with another person and periodically ran away from home. But while the latter adapted to his new life and became a responsible husband and father, Kumari's spouse never sleeps with her and eventually abandons her at her parents' place. The marriage is over before it even begins.

The last section of the film shifts to Kumari, who returns to her work as a farmhand but finds out that it can never be the same again. The local women begin to gossip, and she is soon accused of having loose morals. Rather than taking her side, they band against her and blame her for the failure of her marriage. Their reaction becomes a tacit endorsement of the patriarchal codes that hold women responsible for the ills that befall men. Kumari stoically bears this calumny, but it is too much for her frail father. In the closing scene, he erupts angrily at the go-between and blames him for the scandal.

As they wrangle over the terms of the divorce they will now arrange, Kumari, who had been privy to their conversation, standing unseen by the door, comes forward and tells them not to quarrel. There has been, she tells them, no consummation, and hence no marriage: "We are not man and wife." It is the moment of truth, and we admire the strong and forthright manner with which Kumari makes it known. She, who has barely spoken in the film and kept her eyes lowered for the most part, now asserts herself and proves that the whole experience has only made her stronger. Visually, her sudden emergence from her room and doorway, from invisibility to visibility, defines her as a woman who will not play the victim anymore. She will not hide from society and shed tears in shame, nor will she merely stand in the doorway and let others debate her future. She confronts the reality of her situation and makes it public. In the process, she breaks free from all attempts to judge her. She will only be judged by herself and on her terms. Thus Kumari successfully redefines herself as woman and individual and frees herself from the fakeness of a non-marriage where the term "wife" had become meaningless.

Chinnu Amma (The Housewife): Achieving Motherhood

In this third story, Chinnu Amma craves motherhood, but so far all her offspring have died shortly after their birth. When the film opens, she seems to have accepted her condition. It is at this point that her old school friend, Nara Pillai, appears in her life (Figure 13). He now lives in Tamil Nadu with his wife and children, and the signs of his material prosperity are writ large on his clothes and in his general bearing. As the two exchange fond memories, it becomes evident that Pillai had a crush on Chinnu Amma but she—protective of her virginity—warded him off with the understanding that they could have sex after her marriage.

Fig. 13. *Naalu Pennungal.* Chinnu Amma and Nara Pillai.

Pillai is sad to learn of her dashed hopes of motherhood and how, as a woman, she is held accountable for her childlessness. However, there is enough medical evidence to prove that it is really her husband who is the cause. Pillai is confident that with another man, she would be able to conceive successfully—the other man being none other than himself. This way they would not only enjoy their deferred sex, but it would produce the child she covets. The resolution of the story hinges on the question whether Chinnu Amma will accept or decline his offer—a decision fraught with obvious moral implications.

Chinnu Amma critiques the social construction of motherhood and how it defines the status of a woman within a society deeply invested in family values. The stigma of childlessness can be crippling in such a culture. Almost invariably, it is the woman who gets the blame. In fact, Chinnu Amma frequently uses the word *"fault"* to describe her situation—another example of how women internalize the judgment of others. She knows deep down that the term does not really apply to her, but she has been taught to embrace it, in deference to her spouse.

Her husband apparently does not like to bring up the whole business—especially his culpability—but simply invokes God's will if pressed. Emboldened by Pillai's words, Chinnu Amma confronts him and claims that she may not be responsible for her childlessness. It is a bold move and, in response, her husband asks her brusquely if he is the one at fault. We immediately sense his defensiveness because he cannot bear to have his male sexual prowess questioned under any circumstances. "Fault," as used by him, implies its complete irrelevance when applied to him, and Chinnu Amma, as wife and woman, knows that only too well.

Later, in another scene, when she asks why he seems upset, he claims he has been angry with himself ever since she suggested that he is the cause of her condition. It is his way of making her feel guilty for having broached the subject in the first place. She immediately obliges by regressing to her role of the compliant and self-sacrificing wife. "It must be my fault then," she reassures him.

Given what transpires between Chinnu Amma and her husband, it is not surprising that she turns away Pillai. She is much too insecure to fight the patriarchy and its attempts to control her. Nor can she reject the double standards imposed on her by a society that has been patently unfair to her kind. The shot of her standing in the doorway, bidding Pillai farewell, reveals her barely concealed desire for him. Taught to repress such illicit desires and their forbidden pleasures, she chooses to live out her repressions by conforming to her prescribed role of the morally upright married woman.

The film has a brief coda that is disorienting at first. During the goodbye scene, the camera cuts from Chinnu Amma at the doorway to a slow pan that stops at a young woman in a pink *sari*. She is in a room with other women, listening to a female voice speaking off-screen. The voice states how if she had had a child, he would have looked after her in her old age, but what mattered to her most was keeping her honor and virtue intact. We realize the voice belongs to the elderly Chinnu Amma, who has just narrated the story we saw on film and now seeks to justify her choice to reject Pillai. Despite her attitude of moral righteousness, her tone is wistful and suggests the opposite—a sense of regret has remained with her. Also, the fact that she needs to tell her story (often?) is in itself a sign that she can't let go of the past. Chinnu Amma is doomed—like so many others—to live out the lie behind which she hides. However, the coda manages to offer a glimmer of hope. The juxtaposition of past and present, of old age and youth, suggests that the new generation of women in their colorful *saris* and bright faces will not falter when it is time for them to decide. Hopefully, they will choose passion over a deadening morality and not remain trapped in the doorway.

Nitya Kanyaka (The Spinster): A Life Outside Marriage

Nitya Kanyaka's alternate title could be *The Woman Who Got Left Behind* because the film traces the gradual marginalization of the female protagonist Kamakshi until she is all by herself at the end. Her family consists of her widowed mother, two younger sisters, Subhadra and Sarojam, and a younger brother. While all the siblings are unwed at the start of the film, she has priority over them because she is the eldest daughter. The opening scene, in fact, alludes to a marriage proposal for her. Our first glimpse of Kamakshi is of her standing at the rear of the room just behind her mother, who is framed by the doorway (Figure 14). The women wait expectantly while the prospective bridegroom, his father and the matchmaker confer with the brother. But Kamakshi loses out to the prettier Subhadra, who puts her head around the door and gets herself noticed. She is thus chosen over Kamakshi. When the remaining two siblings are subsequently married off and the mother dies, Kamakshi—now in her thirties—moves in with Subhadra and her family. But when people spread false rumors about her relationship with her brother-in-law, Kamakshi goes back to her old home to live alone.

Gopalakrishnan returns to the subject of marriage and its centrality in shaping the lives and identities of women. Kamakshi's gradual isolation occurs in a society where marriage defines a woman's sense of legitimacy and self-worth. The unwed daughter invariably finds herself stigmatized and socially estranged. As her youngest sister tells Kamakshi, it would be unthinkable for a woman to live "without the help of a man." Kamakshi demonstrates

Fig. 14. *Naalu Pennungal.* Kamakshi and her mother in the doorway.

at the end that she can do exactly that. The film does not present her as a firebrand feminist but as a woman whose experiences make her stronger until she achieves a new sense of selfhood and independence.

The opening sequence of *Nitya Kanyaka* encapsulates—spatially and otherwise—some of the key issues in the film. The men occupy the living room and the daughters their segregated space inside the house, while the mother stands framed in the doorway between the two groups. Such a division of space in relation to gender eloquently expresses the power hierarchy. The women wait expectantly for the negotiations to produce a positive result, but they have virtually no say in the matter. Their silence sets them apart from the men, who are defined as the arbiters of women's fates.

As the camera pans from one end of the room to the other, the conversation centers on the state of post-independence India: the lack of future planning; the ineptness of leaders; and the urgent need for credibility, confidence and foresight. The moving camera is carefully cued so the words are associated with those to whom they apply the most. For example, the reference to the absence of planning is visually linked to the women and their indeterminate future (especially with regard to Kamakshi), while the allusion to limited foresight prompts a tilt-down to the man who will impulsively choose Subhadra over Kamakshi because of her good looks.

The men are shown discussing politics because it is a male thing as well as a convenient icebreaker for the two families, who are trying to get to know each other. However, Gopalakrishnan's wonderful mise-en-scène turns their conversation into a critique of their own limitations and shortcomings and implicates the state as well. The latter is held accountable for allowing women to be the victims of a chauvinistic ideology based on gender inequality. Thus the private and the public come together. Kamakshi's predicament as a woman is placed within the larger context of India's—and specifically Kerala's—history since independence. And we, viewers, are asked to reflect on both past and present in order to achieve a historical awareness of her condition. The sudden expansion of space and time, therefore, gives Kamakshi and her story a whole new context and affects our perception of her place in the film.

After her rejection by the man who becomes her brother-in-law, it does not take long for Kamakshi to discover that she is being gradually sidelined within her family. Despite an outward show of support from her brother and sisters, she knows she must eventually fend for herself. During Subhadra's wedding, she is asked not to participate in the rituals because it could bring bad luck. Her sense of ostracism is compounded by the alienation she feels when Subhadra and her husband come to visit. The dark-skinned, plainly dressed Kamakshi is contrasted with her fair-skinned, beautiful sister who wears bright, colorful *saris*. The mother's preference for Subhadra is only too evident in these scenes. Kamakshi is turned away as if she were an outsider when she eavesdrops on a conversation between mother and sister. Shots of her working in the kitchen while Subhadra lounges around doing nothing further confirm her diminution in status. She is even berated by the mother for taking too long to prepare the ingredients for their guests' meal. Kamakshi reacts to these signs of her otherness within the family by shedding tears of self-pity in bed at night. But she also displays her strong feelings of resentment. Any hint of physical intimacy between Subhadra and her husband, although behind closed doors, is cause for jealousy and bitterness. There is even a scene where she suddenly provokes her sister by calling her spouse a lazy slob. This is a new Kamakshi: angry—even vengeful—and grappling with emotions she has not experienced before.

As Kamakshi's chances of finding a husband fade—there is a poignant moment when she gazes at her aging face in the mirror—and her remaining siblings are married off, she becomes the source of her mother's deep and abiding anxiety. She must, therefore, live with her sense of guilt for causing the latter's mental and physical distress (for she soon falls ill). Even on her deathbed, Kamakshi's mother does not stop worrying about her future. Having run out of hope, she finally attributes her daughter's "tragedy" to the machinations of fate. Kamakshi is thus indirectly blamed for having brought upon herself the curse of an unfavorable destiny. The mother dies unconsoled, although her children assure her that they will always be there for their sister.

In the final section of the film, as Kamakshi lives with Subhadra and her family, she feels increasingly unwanted and unwelcome in her new liminal space. However, there is a redeeming feature: her love for her nieces is amply reciprocated. She treats them as her own children and thus experiences the vicarious pleasure of surrogate motherhood. It is also at this time that she receives an unexpected apology from her brother-in-law. "What I did to you is unpardonable," he abruptly confesses. Although genuinely contrite, his admission does little good except to salve his own conscience. What occasions this sudden avowal of guilt is his recognition that he is largely responsible for Kamakshi's dependent status, but that does not change anything. In fact, from now on things get steadily worse as people maliciously gossip about her, making Subhadra resent her presence. Kamakshi discovers that her hidebound, orthodox society will not tolerate her otherness as an unmarried woman. Earlier, a man solicited her openly when she was walking by herself.

Kamakshi's final displacement takes her back to her old house, which is now empty. The film thus returns to where it began, except that the woman who waited expectantly behind her mother for a man to decide her future is now fully empowered to make her own choices and create her own home. The prospect of living alone for the rest of her life does not deter her one bit. When her youngest sister invites her to live with her family, Kamakshi tells her that she now enjoys living by herself. Nor does she care about what people think or say. She compares herself to the pillar of a house, which must be strong in order to hold up the structure. This declaration of strength and independence marks Kamakshi's journey from the woman who stood literally in the doorway to one who has reclaimed her space and made it her own. She is no longer the woman who got left behind but a woman who has defined herself on her own terms.

There is a coda to the film in which we see Kamakshi turn away a man who knocks on her door at night. She had apparently encouraged him to visit her but now attributes it to a momentary aberration—"I wavered." She thus proves to herself that she can transcend her sexual yearnings and free herself from this last vestige of dependence on men. Her last words in the film, addressed to him but more to herself, are, "It should not be impossible that a woman can make her life without a man." Is Kamakshi merely repressing her desires to make a larger political statement about her newfound freedom as a woman? Or is she articulating a deep-felt need to truly assert her independence? The film leaves the question open.

Kallante Makan (*The Thief*): Taking on the Man's Role

This poignant story—the very first in *Oru Pennum Randaanum*—of a father-son relationship opens with a woman in the doorway. This time, it is the mother who watches the father, Neelantan, embrace their nine-year-old son, Kunjunni, on his release from jail. The man is a thief by necessity because thievery is his only means of supporting his impoverished family, and this occupation has resulted in multiple arrests and long spells behind bars. Soon Neelantan is taken into custody again for threatening his neighbor with burglary. A petition signed by local residents, complaining of his criminal acts, leads to his arrest.

The emotional core of the film derives from Kunjunni's attachment to his father, whose absence he keenly feels. He also has to suffer the put-downs of his classmates and locals who openly call him "son of a thief." Pining for his father's release, he's resolved to make him stop stealing—the only way he can make him stay with him. Besides, as he tells his mother, it is wrong to steal. The father does sneak in one night but only after breaking out of jail. He burgles his neighbor's house and with the stolen money buys his son new clothes and arranges a sumptuous lunch for him. But he remains in hiding, and Kunjunni never sets eyes on him. However, the son eventually catches on and is almost inconsolable because his father has stolen again and will be taken from him once again.

The mother, framed in the doorway, is a passive witness in the opening scene, but she soon finds herself occupying the space reserved for the man in the family. She thus crosses more than a physical threshold as she assumes the combined role of father and mother, becoming the source of her son's material and emotional well-being. She repeatedly comforts her forlorn son like a mother would but also engages in hard labor, which is generally identified with men. We see her stripping the husk from coconuts to earn a few paltry coins for their survival. We also find out that she's been soliciting friends and benefactors for Neelantan's release. The film thus defines her as a woman who exceeds the responsibilities traditionally associated with her sex. Since Neelantan's arrest and long incarceration are inevitable at the end of the film, she knows she will have to raise her son with the same tenacity and determination she has already displayed. She has, in fact, successfully transformed herself into Gopalakrishnan's ideal nurturing woman and provider. And she will never stand in the doorway again—the space has expanded to accommodate her new self.

Oru Koottukaran (Two Men and a Woman): A Woman Off-Screen

Oru Koottukaran introduces the concept of the threesome that will reach its full form in *Pankiyamma (One Woman, Two Men)*. Since the male protagonists are close friends, they have no desire to compete over the same woman, but they become partners in a series of deliberations that concern her and her future.

Krishnankutty, a college student, lives off his uncle, who supports him financially in the hope that Krishnankutty will one day wed his daughter. His lawyer friend, a few years older than him, is like a big brother who counsels him whenever he's in trouble. When the film opens, Krishnankutty is in serious trouble, having got his servant pregnant. She sweeps and cleans for him and belongs to a lower caste. Since the woman is willing to have an illegal abortion, the two friends visit a quack who—for a price—will terminate the fetus. Soon after, Krishnankutty shows up noticeably relieved because the pregnancy was a false alarm. When his friend questions him, he appears to have gotten over his infatuation, but the fact remains that he can't put his mind to his studies and is in danger of failing his exams as usual. If that were to happen again, his uncle would withdraw his support. When Krishnankutty visits his friend at the end of the film, he has startling news. He's not only back with the woman who is now truly pregnant, but he wishes to marry her. He apparently has genuine feelings for her and is ready to face his uncle's wrath and rejection. He is also resigned to failing his exams.

In this minimalist and largely banal narrative based mostly on encounters between the two friends, the nameless woman is conspicuously absent but remains a potent off-screen presence in the film. Her invisibility in itself points to her complete helplessness as the two men decide her fate. We almost sense her presence within a ghostly doorway, where she waits expectantly for the men's verdict. Krishnankutty speaks on her behalf a few times, giving her a voice, but such a mediated, self-serving male point of view can barely do her any justice. As a weak and indecisive youth, he is scarcely able to articulate his own desires and needs. Drawn to her "innocence," as he claims later, he takes full advantage of her naiveté. He also exploits her vulnerability as a member of an "inferior" caste that is associated with degrading labor. She agrees to the abortion only because Krishnankutty promises to marry her in the near future, when he'll hold a job. This would, of course, be an enormous social boost for her, but the cowardly Krishnankutty has no such intentions (and he has no future, in any case, because he routinely fails his exams). He only selfishly wants to save himself from public disgrace. Accordingly, the woman must pay the price, and that too at the hands of a notorious quack. Krishnankutty not only betrays her but also betrays his uncle and the daughter he is expected to wed.

What causes the young man's subsequent change of heart is not fully explained. A sudden surge of feeling for the woman—as he explains to his friend—seems highly suspect. Instead of reigning himself in, the spineless Krishnankutty has now finally gotten her pregnant, and this time her family knows and is putting pressure on him. There is really no way out but to marry her. The task would be made simpler if he could convince himself that he loves her; he would then no longer have to struggle with his conscience. This is precisely what he does by the time the two friends meet. But with no prospects of any kind, his choice is nothing more than an example of his impractical, delusional nature. He may feel good about it but, in reality, he is letting down both himself and the woman. The nameless servant, who never gains voice or face in the film, does gain an ineffectual husband in a sham marriage of convenience.

Pankiyamma (One Woman, Two Men): Politics of the Threesome

In *Pankiyamma*, the woman is not only visible but in full control of the relationship in which she's emotionally and sexually involved with two men. The young and beautiful Pankiyamma (Panki for short) is a coveted object for men who fight over her (Figure 15). She eventually marries the middle-aged landlord, Rama Kurup, who divorces his wife and bequeaths all his estates to her before their marriage. Soon Panki takes a lover—Kuttan Pillai—who is closer to her in age. When Kurup catches them in flagrante, he stabs Pillai and disappears before turning himself in. Meanwhile, Pillai recovers from his

Fig. 15. *Oru Pennum Randaanum*. Panki reads on her porch.

wound and resumes his relationship with Panki. Kurup, on bail, returns to live with her. In the trial that ensues, he is acquitted of attempted murder, but both men are found guilty of other charges and sentenced to three years of rigorous imprisonment.

Gopalakrishnan is careful not to present Panki as a femme fatale who devours and destroys her men. Instead, Kurup and Pillai get the blame for allowing their passions to overcome them. The film has a frame story in which an elderly woman narrates Panki's story to her husband, who apparently never tires of hearing it. She ascribes guilt to the men. Panki's beauty had its allure, but it was the men, after all, who lost their heads over her. Why should she be considered a vile dissembler with no scruples, she argues, when the men are far from being virtuous? She takes Panki's side all along, which is essentially the film's point of view. The frame story thus filters Panki's story through a woman's narrative, which gives it a distinct shape and voice.

Gopalakrishnan sees Panki as a woman who lives naturally and loves naturally.[1] She doesn't choose between her two men but cares for them equally. When called upon to make a deposition at the trial, she is not partial to one over the other (although each would have liked some preference). Similarly, she helps them both with money when they need it. With regard to the question of infidelity, the film presents her extramarital affair as an example of how she doesn't subscribe to conventional morality. She simply follows her instincts to give and accept love. Unlike most of Gopalakrishnan's women, she has a clear conscience and can transcend the expectations and prejudices of her society.

It is the men who come across as inherently jealous, possessive and demanding. From the outset, Panki is shown in relation to Kurup's controlling gaze. When he gives her a red blouse, he wants her to put it on immediately, although she is busy in the kitchen. She gives in and becomes the object of his silent reverie. All he wants to do—he tells her—is sit and look at her. But becoming an object of adoration, Panki discovers, involves having to contend with extreme jealousy and suspicion. Kurup frets if she does not answer him at once and resents her loud laughter; he even wakes up in the middle of the night and imagines someone knocking on their door, such is his fear of losing her to a younger man. Pillai, on the other hand, is more shrewd and scheming and seems to have his eyes on Panki's money. Since he almost died out of love for her, he expects some form of recompense. He is disappointed when she stays neutral in her deposition at court.

In the last section of the film, the two men find themselves serving their sentences in the same jail. They gradually lose their animosity and become friends. On their release, both—but especially Pillai—claim they have scores to settle with Panki, the source of their misery. But she has a surprise in store for them when they visit her. Not only is there a man living with her, but he is the father of her child. Panki has moved on with her life and, once again, shows no guilt in having taken on a new lover. In the end, it is not she but Kurup and Pillai, the two ineffectual males, who receive their comeuppance.

The passionate, warm-hearted and canny Panki is unique in Gopalakrishnan's oeuvre and the most potent example of a woman who will not let herself be framed by any doorway or, for that matter, any relationship. She reinvents herself continually and asserts her freedom of choice and independence. In relation to the other women, she's the most high-spirited and upbeat. Nothing seems to faze her, and her animated laugh resounds in the film. The others—for the most part—strive to be strong, even defiant, but can never attain her zest for life. Panki thus embodies a certain form of emancipation that eludes these women whose stories circulate within the familiar tropes of displacement, otherness and—in the cases of Kunju Pennu and Kamakshi—a search for home without a clear sense of resolution. But Panki seems unstoppable, letting nothing confine or limit her ardor for life and passion. She thus symbolizes hope for all women, regardless of their individual contexts, who seek to cross every threshold in their quest for freedom and selfhood.

Chapter 7

MAKING THE IMAGINARY REAL: *ANANTARAM, MATHILUKAL* AND *NIZHALKKUTHU*

In the 1980s, there was a shift in Gopalakrishnan's work as he sought to locate otherness in an interior space that he associated with the creative process. It was an extension of his lifelong fascination with human interiority, which was now given a new context: creativity. *Mathilukal* (*The Walls*, 1989) and *Anantaram* (*Monologue*, 1987) feature men who, like many of his protagonists, are physically or psychically displaced but invent and inhabit a complex imaginary world, thus reconfiguring their sense of difference. Such is their immersion in this world that it acquires a perfectly convincing reality that is more compelling than the one that lies outside it, thus leaving the question open as to what constitutes the real. We have already seen how in *Mukhamukham* an entire community collectively authored an image that, at the end of the film, turned out to be more real than the man on which it was based. In these films, as well, the imaginary comes to take the place of the real and exceeds it in terms of veracity. In each case the power of the human mind and its creative potential is affirmed.

In *Mathilukal*, Basheer is a political activist and author who finds himself in jail, cut off from the contexts in which he functions as a writer. The film focuses on how he engages with the creative process from within while virtually isolated from the rest of the world. *Anantaram* also describes an inner process. Its subject is a young man with a serious psychological condition who invents alternate realities that are at the heart of his complex narratives. To these films of the '80s, one must add Gopalakrishnan's *Nizhalkkuthu*, made in 2002, which features an older man—an outsider in his community—whose power of empathy enables him to reinvent the story he listens to in the second half of the film. If, so far, we've encountered men who were actively engaged in the creative process, in this later film, the protagonist serves as the receiver or recipient of an oral narrative that triggers a radical rewriting of the story. Like the earlier films, *Nizhalkkuthu* also makes us reflect on the dividing line between art and life and between real and imaginary as well as the question about the nature of reality.

In all three films, the engagement with the imaginary is equated with freedom and liberation. The protagonists rise above the limits of their circumscribed lives through the creative process they initiate. In each case (but especially in *Mathilukal* and *Nizhalkkuthu*) the men experience a form of release that evokes transcendence. It enables them to redefine their sense of self and freedom and reevaluate the material realities of their lives. Thus, in relation to the previous films in which both otherness and emancipation were often defined in social and historical terms, here the emphasis shifts almost exclusively to an interior realm.

Anantaram: Same Story Told Twice

In *Anantaram*, Ajayan, a college student in his early twenties, is a schizophrenic who cannot distinguish fact from fiction. The film is structured around a pair of parallel narratives that are authored by him. As he relates the story of his life through a voice-over, he singles out—via a series of flashbacks—those events that he believes can explain the actions that have brought him to the point where the narrative begins. In effect, he tells us the same story twice but includes different episodes and a different set of emphases each time. Since he maintains a confessional tone right to the end, he assumes an audience that we constitute.

As the film unfolds, we realize that Ajayan is in the middle of a profound crisis that he tries to resolve by justifying the choices he has made. The first narrative purportedly tries to give us an objective account of events. The second seeks to provide a rationale that would explain his situation. Accordingly, this second narrative is much more subjective, as Ajayan tries to dredge up the hidden sources of his trauma. It helps us retrospectively fill in the gaps that the first version has repressed. Both narratives, then, are equally important and complement each other.

As in *Mukhamukham*, a central question in the film revolves around whether we can ever really know Ajayan using these double narratives. Ajayan is skeptical himself. In fact, both stories end with his admission that each account is incomplete and that much remains unsaid. These untold versions could include his own as well as those by others who know him well. The film ends with *anantaram*—"And then"—a storytelling device that suggests that there is no closure for this process. Ajayan's story will thus continue to unfold through multiple narratives, denying us a single, comprehensive truth. It points to a fundamental issue in epistemology: the unknowability of the human psyche.

Ajayan's mental condition compounds the problem. We have a narrator who is not merely unreliable but whose unreliability is pathological in nature. Even the objective account of the first narrative is open to question, since the facts he presents could very well be fiction. For Gopalakrishnan, this inability to keep the two separate is not exclusive to Ajayan but applies, in general, to human subjectivity (we recall *Mukhamukham* in this respect). However, in Ajayan's case, it acquires an extreme form due to his illness.

Instead of turning *Anantaram* into an exclusively psychoanalytic study of the Other, Gopalakrishnan treats Ajayan's compulsion to narrate as a creative act. As he puts it, "When there is a method to madness, it becomes creation."[1] Ajayan's need to make sense of his life by giving it a voice and shape invokes storytelling and thus creativity. It provides Gopalakrishnan with a chance to reflect on the creative process itself, specifically in the context of pathology. He claims that the structure of the film simulates the very process of creating fiction, which he breaks down into "perception, selection, and arrangement of experience."[2] This is what Ajayan does, in essence: he first assimilates the events in his life, then selects those he would like to retain in his memory before arranging and presenting them in a certain order to suit his personal agenda. Thus what he offers us in the name of truth is an elaborate construction that he believes will explain the logic underlying his crisis. In reality, it is only a recasting of the actual events, which are governed by selective recall and subjectively determined to justify his actions. Given his schizophrenia, such an attempt at creating a rationale is necessarily conditioned by his irrationality.

Ajayan's First Narrative: Illicit Passion

In the first narrative, Ajayan seeks to provide us with a scenario that would explain his psychological makeup as an outsider as well as focus on the facts of the crisis that has undermined his hold on reality. One of the key images in this early section is that of young Ajayan curled up in the fetal position, pressed up against a wall, occupying one-third of a hospital bed. It alludes to his illegitimacy and his abandonment by his mother at birth, which generated a lifelong sense of insecurity. He was subsequently adopted and brought up by a doctor but was never able to forgive his mother or overcome his bitter hatred for her. At one point, he even speaks of strangling her. This sense of rejection, accompanied by violent antagonistic feelings, is one of the possible sources of Ajayan's psychosis and also partly explains the problematic nature of his future relationships with women.

As he grows up into a teenager, Ajayan proves himself to be quite exceptional in almost every respect, which also sets him apart from others.

As a young teenager, he excels in school as well as in sports and music. Out swimming with his friends, he manages to stay under water longer than anybody else. But despite his accomplishments, he barely receives any compliments or encouragement, except at home. At school, Ajayan's precociousness draws only grudging approval from his teacher, who considers him essentially an upstart and show-off. In a world of mediocrity, he repeatedly encounters jealousy and resentment, which make him deeply cynical about fairness and justice.

Ajayan thus grows up convinced that his special gifts will never be appreciated and he will not be treated fairly. It only deepens his sense of marginalization that was instilled at birth. As he states in his voice-over, the distinction of being the best proved to be a curse. Subsequently, as a college student, Ajayan loses the initiative to do well, neither attending classes regularly nor taking exams. We find out in the second half that the problem began when he was still a teenager. His foster-brother, Balu, wonders whether being so brilliant really did Ajayan any good because it prevented him from leading a normal life.

Although the doctor who adopted Ajayan is portrayed as a loving parent, the latter is very self-conscious that he is not the doctor's biological son. He calls him "doctor-uncle," not father, an acknowledgement of his own sense of otherness within the family. When the doctor dies suddenly, Ajayan, who is studying in the city, is deliberately notified after the funeral is over. This upsets him deeply. Balu explains that it would have been inappropriate for him to participate in the last rites. This only reinforces Ajayan's feeling of exclusion, which, in turn, further complicates his sense of self and identity. He also learns how appearances can be very deceptive; the doctor is like his father but not his father, Balu is like his brother but not his real brother and those who admire his talents only pretend to do so while secretly resenting his success. This gap that he perceives between appearance and reality widens to such an extent that the neurotic Ajayan is hopelessly lost in it.

The crisis in Ajayan's life is triggered by Balu's marriage to Sumangala. During the ceremony, we notice his rapt, intent gaze directed at her. The camera slowly zooms twice to his furrowed brows to underline this fixation. When he is home for the holidays, he literally cannot stop looking at her. During dinner, he forgets to eat, either staring into space or at her, totally self-absorbed. The intensity of his gaze and his apparent lack of discretion disconcert both Sumangala and Balu—the latter even asks what he is staring at. But she is affected the most. When Ajayan abruptly decides to return to his hostel although his classes have not begun, he asks for her hand and plants a kiss on her palm. His look this time is unmistakably one of desire and yearning.

Incestuous feelings for one's sister-in-law, especially within the conservative middle class Malayali family, cannot but generate profound inner trauma.

Gopalakrishnan describes it as Ajayan's "impossible relationship," which dooms him to irresolution, guilt and internal agony.[3] At the same time, he makes us question the nature of this infatuation. Is Ajayan merely in the grip of a forbidden passion, or is it another manifestation of his deeply conflicted, neurotic personality? The dislocating nature of his gaze suggests that all is not well and that the obsession with Sumangala may have some other, hidden source. Either way, such illicit desire also acquires a logic of its own when placed within the contexts of Ajayan's illegitimacy and his marginalized status. He is, as it were, incapable of falling in love except outside society's prescribed, normative standards. This is only consistent with his social and psychological condition. In this sense, Ajayan, the outsider, seems destined to live out these impossible scenarios, irrespective of their nature and origin.

Gopalakrishnan cuts from the hand-kissing scene to Ajayan in his college hostel, where he is about to write a letter to Balu. We hear its contents on the soundtrack. It is, as we suspect, a confession of his love for Sumangala—"I burn all over with this forbidden passion"—that ends with a plea for his brother's forgiveness. Because Balu has always loved him, Ajayan is overcome with guilt and masochistically demands his own punishment: "I long for you to be cruel to me."

We subsequently see Sumangala weeping over the letter while Balu tries to console her. Gopalakrishnan then cuts back to Ajayan sitting at his desk while his voice-over informs us that he couldn't even write a line, knowing full well the consequences of such a letter falling into Balu's hands. The two scenes back-to-back reinforce how Ajayan can invent scenarios that, at first, seem authentic, only to be later explained as a projection. His blank sheet and pen allude to his capacity for authoring such fantasies, which he now acknowledges as being such but will gradually accept as real. His admission makes us evaluate what we have witnessed (and heard) so far during this first rendition of his past. We wonder how much has been fabricated, omitted and revised in this seemingly objective account.

As if sensing our ambivalence, Ajayan declares at the end of his narrative that his story remains incomplete, thus necessitating a second one, which will, hopefully, provide a convincing rationale for his derailed emotional life. It is significant that these words are heard over what is one of the most despairing scenes in the film: Ajayan's attempt at suicide, apparently caused by his guilty passion. We see students gather outside his hostel room, bang on his door and peer through the glass panel on it. The locked door and his absence from the frame suggest that both Ajayan and his narrative have reached an impasse. The students become our stand-in, representing our craving for knowledge that can be fulfilled only by a second narrative.

Ajayan's Second Narrative: The Roots of Psychosis

This second narrative starts with Ajayan going back even further in time, to his six-year-old self. We first see him in a room filled with stuffed birds and a large grandfather clock. As it strikes twelve, he begins to rotate clockwise, in cue with the beat of the pendulum, until he collapses on the ground. It becomes an almost ritualistic transition from clock time to a time-free realm—the realm of memories. In short, as Ajayan falls, he also falls out of time.

The voice-over belongs to the same grown-up Ajayan of the first story, who tells us about his lonely childhood spent at the mercy of three sinister and tyrannical servants who rule over the house when the doctor and Balu are away. The cook, Raman Nair, eats almost everything he prepares; Mathai, the driver, spends all his time repairing the car but cannot make it run; and the nameless compounder sleeps in the dispensary. In Ajayan's account, the servants assume almost diabolical proportions as his tormentors, brutally enforcing discipline. On one occasion, the compounder severely canes him for disrupting his afternoon siesta and calls him a "bastard," implying that the boy's illegitimacy could be more complex than what the first narrative made it out to be. It also raises the related question of discrimination—would Ajayan have been beaten so viciously if he had been the doctor's biological son? The unusual circumstances of his birth and adoption seem to make him vulnerable to such crippling abuse—more proof of his status as an outsider within the household.

The servants play another role in the boy's life: they feed him bizarre tales that undermine his precarious hold on reality. Ajayan's tendency, as an adult, to confuse the real with the imaginary could have its source in such moments of utter disorientation. The three men could thus be said to contribute to his psychotic condition—especially when they manage to instill fear in him through their concoctions. For example, when Ajayan sees a strange woman cross the verandah of the house on a rainy night, he is told she is a *yakshi*—a seductive female spirit. He flees to the safety of his bed, where he develops a fever. As with all of Ajayan's recollections, the issue of authenticity remains problematic. The same servants, at other points in the film, are extremely kind and warm-hearted toward him. As perverse authority figures, are they a projection of his insecurities and repressed anger?

Balu, a relatively minor figure in the first half, plays a prominent role in this second narrative. In a film full of shifting perspectives, he is the only stable center. Consistently rational and clear-headed, he embodies a normalcy that acts as a counterpoint to Ajayan's schizophrenia. He is the hardworking, diligent medical student who subsequently becomes a very successful doctor, the pride of his community and the coveted husband of the local women. He is repeatedly held up to the teenage Ajayan as the paragon of excellence he should emulate. As the latter begins to neglect his studies and succumbs increasingly to apathy and inertia, he is made conscious of his inferiority and incompetence. Reprimanded for not studying, the doctor even asks, "Don't you want to be like Balu?" This makes Ajayan jealous and resentful. When, later, the boy jocularly threatens to "spoil" Balu's marriage, the significance of this remark is not lost on us.

The failure to conform to his foster-brother's high standards comes back to haunt Ajayan when the doctor suddenly dies. Balu tells him that it grieved his father that he could not rise to his expectations. Ajayan thus has to shoulder the double guilt of having let down his father as well as having contributed to his untimely death. This burden, which he must carry for the rest of his life, only deepens his psychosis.

The Advent of Nalini

Having provided us with a new set of contexts that relate to his childhood and later years and that may explain his state of crisis, the college-going Ajayan now introduces us to Nalini, who suddenly appears in his life out of nowhere. She shows up one day while he is waiting at the bus stop and looks at him intently out of the window before the bus departs. She continues to make these appearances, always associated with the same bus, the same bus stop and the same gaze while Ajayan begins to wait for her. Finally, one day she gets off and greets him by name. She claims she knew he would be waiting because, as she puts it enigmatically, "Love needs no words." She then catches another bus and disappears.

What becomes immediately apparent is the fact that Nalini is identical to Sumangala in every respect and played by the same actress. But Ajayan is alluding to a time when Balu was still single and there was no Sumangala in their lives. Nalini is thus a wholly separate individual. However, her subsequent interactions with Ajayan make her more and more of an unreal presence, her corporeality always suspect. She seems to hover in a liminal space, at times taking on the concrete attributes of a real person but, more often than not, appearing as a figment of Ajayan's hyperactive, troubled imagination. She is thus real and imaginary at the same time. Initially, Gopalakrishnan creates this duality by repeatedly placing her in the everyday, banal world of bus stops, buses and their constant movements. He provides a core of realism to these early encounters and thus complicates the issue of Nalini's identity because she exists in real time and space. At the same time, he alludes to the power of Ajayan's creative mind, which can convincingly invent a woman.

As the narrative unfolds, Nalini is increasingly defined as a fantasy-object through whom Ajayan wishes to justify his infatuation with Sumangala and, thereby, exorcize the terrible sin of incest. As per the scenario he creates, his romance with Nalini, which began at the bus stop, ended abruptly one day when she vanished from his life and reappeared as Sumangala, his sister-in-law. Thus Ajayan's obsessive gaze and his impassioned kiss in the first narrative become plausible. They cannot be ascribed to an illicit desire because Sumangala is none other than old flame Nalini, who happens to have married Balu. This is the rationale with which Ajayan hopes to address what was left unsaid in the film's first half and, thereby, free himself from his all-consuming remorse and guilt. It also results in a series of self-interrogations via Nalini as Ajayan seeks to confront the fears and anxieties that have plagued him all his life. Thus, the invention of Nalini serves another crucial function—to begin a complex dialogue with himself that takes him into the deepest recesses of his mind.

Ajayan's initial representation of Nalini links her to an ideal, chaste love that has nothing to do with physical passion. And yet the woman we see in the film is attractive and sensual. He makes Nalini allude to love as an abstract idea from time to time, but it is never convincing. We sense a struggle in Ajayan, who seeks to disarm and disguise his strong desire for Sumangala by aligning it with platonic love. His passion for her can then be denied and rendered safe, but he never quite succeeds because his powerful attraction to Nalini is not rooted in mere abstractions.

Nalini subsequently visits Ajayan in his hostel and also shows up on the beach, both times wearing a bright blue *sari*. On the first occasion, her material presence is so strong that Ajayan fears that he will get into trouble for letting a woman into his room. She reproaches him for being cowardly and then adds coyly that she expected her lover to be "the bravest and strongest of men." It becomes a form of self-chastisement because Nalini provides Ajayan with an opportunity to admit to his inadequacies and shortcomings. By confronting them vis-à-vis a woman, he also acknowledges the primary source of his many insecurities: his illegitimacy and abandonment. It remains to be seen if he can rise to Nalini's challenge and prove that he has what she looks for in a man.

The meeting on the beach is meant to contrast Nalini's earlier materiality with her dream-like state as she suddenly appears out of thin air, apparently to fulfill Ajayan's yearning (Figure 16). Swathed in the same blue *sari*, she is real enough—holding his hand and walking with him on the sand. But we also sense her insubstantial quality, which culminates in her sudden disappearance. Thus the two scenes underline her enigmatic nature and the duality within which she functions in Ajayan's life.

The enigma deepens when Nalini's father shows up at Ajayan's hostel and asks him to stay away from his daughter because he is about to arrange her marriage to a man with good prospects. Just when we are tempted to accept

Fig. 16. *Anantaram*. Nalini and Ajayan on the beach.

the scene as unequivocally real (given its strong realism), Nalini, in the very next scene, throws off Ajayan—and us—by revealing that her father has been dead for seven years. Utterly confused, he asks the question we ask as well: "Whom should I believe?" Her reply—"That's up to you"—defines the premise of the film and our position as spectators.

If we accept that Nalini's father is dead, then Ajayan's meeting with him is clearly a fantasy provoked by his sense of inadequacy and inability to live up to the expectations of both her and her father. Her earlier gripe that he is not brave or strong enough is confirmed by the father, who declares him a failure with no future, unfit to wed his daughter. Ajayan's anxiety attack stems from his extremely low self-esteem, which makes him fear that he will lose the woman he loves. It is another manifestation of his larger insecurities, which revolve around loss, abandonment and exclusion. The fact that he articulates such anxiety through his invention of Nalini's father reveals the terrible guilt he harbors for indirectly causing his foster-father's death.

But Ajayan also finds a way out by having Nalini expose the father's visit as a hoax, which frees him from his humiliation and also ensures that he will not lose her. After all, he desperately needs Nalini, especially her nurturing presence and empowering love. If his unconditional faith in her were to waver for even a moment, it would erode the very foundations of her existence, making it impossible for him to sustain her reality. But he finds himself constantly struggling with his self-doubts and sense of inferiority, which threaten to destabilize the fantasy has authored. Nalini's sudden disappearance after their meeting on the beach suggests that this is indeed what has transpired. Nalini has vanished, and Ajayan goes in search of her, certain that he can trace her to where she lives. He does indeed meet a woman who has a similar name, but she is not Nalini. The very attempt to find proof of her existence suggests his loss of faith in his creation and his inability to invest in the imaginary.

At the end of the first narrative, Ajayan attempted suicide; now, with Nalini gone, we see him sprawled on his hostel bed in a deathlike posture brought on by his immersion in drugs. The last section of the film examines Ajayan's post-Nalini life, when he is back home, living once again with Balu and Sumangala.

Although Ajayan seems stable at first, we see his look of disbelief and yearning when Sumangala wears a blue *sari* that is identical to the one worn by Nalini on the beach. When Balu returns home for lunch, Ajayan seems agitated and claims that he wants to talk to him. We then hear Balu ask him whether he has taken his medicine. This is a pivotal moment in the film because we learn for the first time that Ajayan is undergoing treatment for what we assume is some form of mental illness.

We see its symptoms manifest shortly afterward when, seeing Sumangala at the door of his room, he becomes deeply upset and calls her "Nalini." Then, with barely suppressed rage and frustration, he tells her that she will not deceive him again. Nalini—now wearing a different *sari*—asks him to stop dreaming and wake up, not realizing that for him dream and reality have fused inextricably. He claims he wants to know the truth—how she, who was Nalini, has now become Sumangala.

That night, he becomes even more agitated despite Balu's attempts to pacify him and make him take his medicine. Finally, he bangs on Balu's bedroom door. When he comes out, we see, from Ajayan's perspective, Sumangala in a flaming red *sari*—the color of desire. It's too much for him, and he asks Balu to send her away—she who, he claims, has consistently betrayed her husband. He even threatens to do it himself, and Balu finally has to restrain Ajayan from entering his room.

It is at this point that Ajayan's voice-over informs us, as it did at the end of the first narrative, that even this version of his life is incomplete because of what he's forgotten to relate or simply doesn't remember. He thus implies that his story will continue to unravel through an endless cycle of narratives without any possibility of closure or of grasping the multifaceted, elusive truth.

The film ends by returning to the six-year-old boy on a flight of steps leading down to the river. He descends to the edge of the water, counting only the odd steps: *one, three, five, seven*. When he reaches the bottom, he climbs back to the top. He descends again, this time counting only the even steps: *two, four, six*. This time, when he reaches the last step, he turns and looks up at the camera.

Gopalakrishnan thus draws our attention to the dual structure of the film—the story has an even version and an odd version. Both are valid. They support each other and anticipate additional narratives that are different and complementary. He then cuts to the empty screen, which contains only one word: *anantaram*. ("And then.") Ajayan's story begins anew as the film ends.

Anantaram, like *Mukhamukham*, continues the discussion about the nature of realism and the representation of reality. Because the film makes us identify deeply with Ajayan's point of view, we experience the imaginary in the guise of the real, defined through a compelling realist aesthetic. Ajayan's fantasies thus acquire a strong, concrete materiality. If realism is said to reveal truth, his very real fabrications (or lies) threaten to undermine this proposition. But Gopalakrishnan suggests that Ajayan's inventions—more real than the real— are intensely truthful within the context of his situation. The latter, in fact, strives to believe in them himself because it is the only way he can resolve his internal crisis. Thus reality is defined in the film as a subjective construction. The schizophrenic Ajayan has boundless freedom to author such realities, which turns the whole thing into a creative endeavor as well as a form of liberation for a man trapped in his sickness.

Mathilukal: Transcending the Walls

Mathilukal is Gopalakrishnan's first film based on a literary source, a novella by Vaikom Mohammed Basheer of the same name, published in 1965. Regarded as a classic of Malayalam literature, it is read virtually by all Malayalis while they are in their teens. Despite its enormous popularity, it had never been filmed because of certain logistical problems (which will soon become clear).

Basheer, the protagonist, is a freedom fighter and well-known writer who is dislocated from his everyday life when he is arrested during Gandhi's 1942 Quit India movement. He finds himself suddenly transformed into an outsider in the alienating precincts of the jail (Figure 17). In his solitude, he establishes contact with Narayani, who lives on the other side of the wall, in the women's prison. She remains invisible, a disembodied voice with whom he communes across the divide. The day they plan to meet at the prison hospital, Basheer is released.

Fig. 17. *Mathilukal.* Basheer in his cell.

Given the idiosyncratic nature of the story, Gopalakrishnan's film functions on a number of levels: as a love story, a prison film, a jail-break film, a film about the Other, a psychoanalytic study of repressed sexuality, a semiotic analysis of the sign, a meditation on liberty and transcendence and a critique of film realism. These categories complement each other and add to the richness of the film. As for the formal challenge of showing a man speaking into thin air for long stretches of time, Gopalakrishnan resolved it by making it part of his larger exploration of the nature of the imaginary.

Like *Anantaram*, *Mathilukal* has two parts. While the first section seems more like a traditional prison film in which we see Basheer in relation to his surroundings and his fellow inmates, the second is about his encounter with Narayani, which leads to his subsequent jailbreak. The two halves are carefully linked in terms of the film's larger thematic and metaphoric structures.

Like Nalini in *Anantaram*, Narayani in *Mathilukal* is given a highly diffuse identity. As Basheer's erotic projection, she is a fantasy-object who fulfills his yearning for a woman. But she could also be a real person with a speaking voice of her own who remains unseen. She is thus presented as real and imaginary, occupying a certain liminal space.

The subject of freedom, which is central to most prison films, is placed here within multiple contexts and thus acquires different meanings. As writer,

Basheer invents a woman who finally becomes so intensely real that he cannot accept his own release from jail because that would mean losing her forever. This ability to create as well as invest his fiction with a compelling reality becomes the key to Basheer's escape from prison. It proves that he can construct and inhabit other realities and break free from all forms of confinement. His liberty thus acquires a certain quality of transcendence. Narayani leads Basheer to this discovery and enables him to locate the source of his freedom within. As in *Anantaram*, their verbal exchanges amount to a form of self-interrogation, making him reflect on issues that range from sexual desire and eroticism to God, love and death. This complex dialogue with himself allows access to his repressed thoughts and feelings. In short, Basheer achieves an empowering self-liberation as he turns more and more inward.

Basheer later speaks philosophically of an all-encompassing jail that incorporates his prison and extends far beyond it. In an existential sense, this is the metaphorical prison of our human condition but also alludes—more importantly—to the one within us. Basheer comes to the realization that, prior to his imprisonment, *he was already in jail*. He had to be physically interned to comprehend this larger notion of confinement and the fact that it relates to all humanity. To experience true freedom, then, one must scale the walls within, which Basheer accomplishes through introspection and self-communion as well as creativity.

But Basheer is also a political activist—the reason why he is behind bars. When he speaks of a "bigger jail" outside, he is also referring to India under British rule. During the course of the film, he will learn how crucial it is to place liberty, as a political concept, within the contexts of creative freedom and personal transcendence. For Gopalakrishnan, the private and the public have never been separate, and they exist here within a complex symbiotic relationship. Basheer's role as political activist in the struggle to free India thus complements his role as artist and eventually enables him to more fully define his sense of humanity.

Reiterating the Real

The first half of *Mathilukal* provides us with the contexts of Basheer's prison life. It is replete with incidental details, anecdotes and stories that may initially appear digressive. It is a long preparatory section that is grounded firmly in realism—in fact, in hyperbolic realism—and allows us to inhabit Basheer's prison world as vividly as possible.

The jail itself is established in all its concrete detail at the very outset. Basheer is transferred from his under trial cell, which he shares with others, to one where he is alone. It overlooks a plot of green. Locked in at night, he is free during the day to wander in the garden or chat with his fellow political prisoners in the adjoining cells. Such proximity to nature and people is offset by the presence of the giant black wall that defines the limits to his freedom. (The gallows are also just around the corner.)

Accorded certain privileges because of his fame as writer, Basheer has access to a wood-fire oven, a pot in which he makes tea with sugar (both forbidden items), a supply of *beedis* and matchsticks, and paper for writing. We see these items repeatedly until they become elements that define and fix him in his space—a physical space from which he will escape one day. Similarly, the film meticulously delineates his daily routine: Basheer wakes up in the morning, has a smoke, fills his bucket from a tap, visits the latrine and takes a bath. The camera describes these chores with an almost documentary-like precision. At times nothing happens in a narrative sense. We watch him smoking, sitting on his mat or standing by the cell door, staring into space. While enforcing his boredom and monotony, such moments heighten our sense of the banal.

In both sections of the film, the camera keeps a certain neutrality, maintaining space-time continuum through long takes and documenting facts from a medium shot perspective, thus insisting on the realism of the scenes. For example, when we see Basheer pace up and down the narrow prison verandah that opens onto the cells, it is shot with almost no cuts, in real space and time that we inhabit with him.

Such a reiteration of the real is done purposefully in relation to the larger discourse of the film. By almost obsessively asking us to focus on the banal, Gopalakrishnan readies us for our encounter with the imaginary and the reality it will acquire. But instead of creating a clear-cut, simplistic opposition between two disparate forms, he places the invention of Narayani within the everyday world of the prison. In other words, the careful marshaling of realism in the first half extends to the second half even as Basheer begins to converse with her. The imaginary is inseparable from the material facts of the setting in which it emerges and with which it coexists almost inextricably. Thus the film does not deny the fact that Narayani could exist behind the wall as an inmate at the women's jail. But by also rendering her invisible and intangible, it erodes our sense of her reality. In short, within the concrete space of the prison, she doubles as a prison inmate and as a projection of Basheer's imagination.

As in *Mukhamukham*, the issue of realism remains complex and problematic throughout the film. For example, despite its strong materiality, the prison, as a place, remains elusive, its layout virtually impossible to determine. There is a sense of walls within walls, of cells leading into cells, all part of a forbidding labyrinthine structure without any apparent beginning or end. In this liminal space that is simultaneously concrete and abstract, real and symbolic, Basheer will encounter his mysterious woman.

Gopalakrishnan also undermines our sense of time in the first half, introducing discreet ellipses that destabilize the narrative. After starting a piece of action, he will often cut abruptly to an event or object off-screen before returning us to the scene. The time that has elapsed is sometimes impossible to fathom. As in *Mukhamukham* and *Anantaram*, the fact that we are never completely sure whether certain events that are "objectively" rendered in the third person have a subjective orientation adds to our confusion. Are they being filtered through Basheer's consciousness? The shots of him writing in his cell reinforce the idea of an active imagination engaged in acts of creativity and are the context for Narayani's subsequent invention. There are also shots of him asleep that invoke dreams and dreaming, making us further question the reality we take for granted.

A complex scene in the film that brings these elements together revolves around a hanging in the jail. On the night it is scheduled to take place, Basheer is shown writing in his cell. We then see him lie down and go to sleep. He is awakened by a guard who tells him that the condemned man is asking for a cup of tea. It is four in the morning, and the hanging will take place in an hour. Basheer obliges, and we watch the guard leave after locking the cell. Basheer remains at the door, looking out, when there is a cut to him sitting down on the mat. He reaches for a *beedi*, which is the cue for another cut that shows him from a different angle, lighting it. These two cuts, however functional, do not reveal how much time has elapsed in relation to their preceding shots.

Basheer now begins to pace up and down in an extended take until finally settling down on the mat again. As he looks toward the door, we hear the sound of a bell—it is time for the hanging. A whole hour has gone by, but the total duration of the sequence is only a few minutes in length. Gopalakrishnan's ability to compress time and also make its passage ambiguous is fully evident here. Since there are shots of Basheer writing as well as sleeping, the scene could also be a fantasy, but it is presented in all its concrete specificity. Once again, our relationship to what we see is left open.

The Social Dynamics of Freedom

Within the reality-unreality of this world, Gopalakrishnan presents us with Basheer the man (as separate from the artist). In order to identify with his creativity in the second half, it is imperative that we get to know him first within the contexts that define his humanity. There is also the underlying assumption that if an artist is to succeed as an artist, he must have impeccable moral credentials. Basheer is put to the test.

Thanks to his good humor and robust personality, Basheer almost immediately forges strong ties with his prison mates. Because he ignores all forms of hierarchies and stays away from any sort of factionalism ("I want to live with everyone amicably"), he gets along well with people from every walk of life, including jail officials and guards. Once he finds himself at the center of this community, his sense of confinement and isolation vanishes. This liberty, in social terms, is no small accomplishment. He has managed to convert a challenging environment into a small haven of human interaction where instead of alienation and loneliness, there is fellow-feeling and mutual sharing. He has metaphorically scaled the walls of his cage. This amounts to what could be described as his first escape.

The formation of this impromptu brotherhood involves gift-giving, which will acquire a special significance in the second half of the film when Basheer and Narayani give each other various items: fried corn, banana chips, fried fish and boiled eggs. But before that happens, Basheer receives gifts from his guards and fellow inmates and, lacking the means, reciprocates not in kind but through his offer of friendship to all and sundry. Whenever he can, he shares whatever comes his way, whether it is tea or *beedis*. Another important aspect of this fraternity entails storytelling. The prisoners confide in Basheer and entrust their narratives to him. He listens intently to what are often harrowing tales of torture, exploitation and deprivation that almost always invoke the body and the violence done to it. In each case, the power of his empathy lets him enter their lives. All these narratives not only reflexively allude to the film itself but prepare us for the final and most complex one that Basheer will author, featuring Narayani. The body will also be central to it, but it will be identified with a different sort of pain: unconsummated desire. Thus the first half of *Mathilukal* is carefully constructed in relation to the key issues of the second half.

The Rose That Won't Bloom

Gopalakrishnan creates a fairly long prelude before Basheer meets Narayani. When a general amnesty for political prisoners is announced, he, like the others, is ecstatic. But he soon finds out that his name is not on the list of those to be freed. The news crushes him. Although he displays his good humor when his fellow prisoners come to say goodbye, once they all leave and he finds himself alone in the complex, he admits to the jailer that he feels a loneliness that he has not known before. It is accompanied by a strange sense of dread and fear. The perennially upbeat Basheer even claims that he has lost his laughter.

As he gets progressively depressed, the man who scaled the walls with his social skills succumbs to their encirclement and becomes a prisoner again. In the past, he never spoke of trying to flee. Now he seems obsessed with the idea and even hatches a plan of escape. In every respect, this is a new Basheer who seems agitated and on the brink of collapse, but for Gopalakrishnan, such a state suggests the exact opposite. Basheer has been emptied out, as it were: purged of his old self and readied for a profound experience. He struggles with this condition because it is new, alienating and ultimately incomprehensible.

The budding rose, a familiar symbol of enlightenment in mystical literature, is used increasingly in the second half of the film to suggest some form of self-awakening. But Gopalakrishnan is careful not to overextend its usage, fully aware of the dangers of turning his protagonist into some dreamy-eyed mystic. We are never allowed to forget that Basheer is a political activist and a man of the world while his status as a writer signals his complex otherness.

The concept of blossoming surfaces in the film quite early. Basheer plants rose bushes after his arrival and nurtures them carefully. Soon the buds begin to blossom, but one holds out, despite all his coaxing. When he complains to the jailer about its stubbornness, he uses the feminine third person: "She's cut up with me. She doesn't respond, she doesn't bloom." Believing that he will be freed with the rest of the prisoners, he says goodbye to "her," sad that he won't see or smell the flower. There are quasi-erotic overtones here that allude to Basheer's yearning for a woman, which is later to be fulfilled by Narayani. But the metaphor of the rose also alludes to a deeper, inner space. We get a hint of this when, struggling with his sense of abandonment after the prisoners leave, he tells the same jailer, "Perhaps I'm not ripe enough." The denial of his freedom is thus located not in an external source but in an interior state. Liberty is linked to an internal condition that can be grasped by the seeker only when he or she is ready within. The recalcitrant rose that is not ripe for blossoming becomes a metaphorical extension of Basheer's situation. Significantly, following Narayani's "appearance," it finally opens its petals. Accordingly, he adopts it as his personal emblem and intends to display it as a mark of identification when he and Narayani meet at the hospital.

A Disembodied Voice

It is while digging in the jail's vegetable garden that Basheer is shown a cement patch on the wall behind which the women's jail is located. He is told that it covers a hole originally made "with the strenuous labor of men yearning for love." It allowed both sexes to have some contact with each other, but any libidinal release was quickly brought to a halt by a corrupt warder who charged men money to peer through the hole. When a prisoner protested, his sentence was extended, and he received 36 whiplashes. The orifice was blocked over with cement. Thus desire was punished with repression and violence.

Basheer reacts to this narrative of thwarted eros by caressing the vagina-shaped patch, then sniffing it. Not only does he empathize with the anguish of the men but also with their longing for a woman. In short, his own repressed desires coupled with his extreme solitude create the perfect setting for his fantasy of Narayani.

It all begins innocuously. Basheer is whistling near the wall. A woman immediately picks up the "signal" from the other side and demands to know his name. He subsequently finds out that she is Narayani, 22 years of age, who has been sentenced to 14 years of rigorous imprisonment (presumably for murder), of which she has completed a year. She informs him that she'll toss a tree branch up in the air to attract his attention in future. Thus the foundation is laid for their dialogues to begin.

Whenever Basheer speaks to Narayani, he is shown standing close to the wall. The camera, in a long take, keeps him mostly in medium shot, emphasizing the reality of his presence as well as the realism that Gopalakrishnan has carefully built up from the start. There are also occasional cutaways to a line of birds on the weather-beaten wall, as if to reaffirm the presence of the material world. Narayani's voice becomes an integral part of this reality. For all practical purposes, she exists, but Gopalakrishnan refuses to cut to a shot of her. She is thus identified exclusively with Basheer's point of view. Since he cannot cross over, the camera remains with him, enforcing the realism but also, simultaneously, making us question its limits because Narayani is invisible.

From their very first conversation, Basheer sexualizes Narayani, and she reciprocates in full measure. Their entire relationship—and especially its eroticism—is, of course, dependent on words. In fact, the only way they can see as well as know each other is through language. On one level, it seems only appropriate that this should be the case, because Basheer is a writer.

When he throws Narayani a rose bush—the first instance of their mutual gift-giving—he first covers it with kisses, then informs her of the fact. She, in turn, tells him that she will pluck the flowers and keep them in her blouse. At one point, Basheer even caresses and kisses the wall as he "massages" her arm (which she claims is out of joint). She, in turn, covers the wall with her kisses and presses her bosom against it. All these acts are verbalized in graphic detail. They even engage in an anatomical exegesis, employing words:

Narayani: The chest?

Basheer: A bit broad.

Narayani: Mine is also broad.

Basheer: My hips are narrow.

Narayani: Mine ... I won't tell.

The prospect of imagining each other's bodies as well as fetishizing body parts is thrilling and poignant at the same time. Denied sight and limited to language, they are both frustrated and aroused by what increasingly becomes a form of verbal foreplay. While the fantasy makes the eroticism more powerful and compelling, the sexualized, invisible body described with words is also, ironically, the body of pain, since it is the site of unfulfilled desire—the desire to see as well as achieve consummation. To imagine each other is, inevitably and sadly, to acknowledge the power of the wall that divides them.

A further irony lies in the fact that while Basheer invents a body for Narayani, she remains, for us, viewers, without a body. Lacking his degree of empathy, we can't visualize her the same way he can. As a disembodied voice, Narayani's reality is dubious in any case, but, given flesh with words, with all their ambiguities and ambivalences, she exists for us within the interstices of existence and nonexistence, reality and nonreality, a strong liminal presence at best. But this is not so for Basheer. For him, Narayani's body becomes intensely real—as real as the prison cell, the trees in the garden and the wall itself. In fact she gradually becomes more real than everything that surrounds him. Finally, her reality acquires such an overpowering quality that, at the end, he is loath to leave the jail. The imaginary thus takes on a vivid concrete shape that blurs the line between the real and the illusory. Basheer cannot tell the difference anymore, just as Ajayan's infatuation with Nalini blinds him. For Gopalakrishnan, this blurring is a vindication of his protagonist's extraordinary creative imagination. To invent Narayani is in itself a tremendous, liberating feat, but by investing her with a more-than-tangible-reality, Basheer fully affirms his power as artist and transcends the walls in his second escape.

Narayani also becomes the source of Basheer's escape from the metaphorical prison within, enabling him to come to terms with some of the key issues in his life. She initiates his complex discourse with himself. As he talks to her, he is essentially talking to himself. What constitutes the most intriguing aspect of this dialogue is Basheer's ability to become a woman. As Narayani, he identifies with a distinctively female point of view (although it is always mediated by his male consciousness). While he broaches subjects such as sexuality and desire, which could be described as inherently masculine, Narayani brings up issues like God, spirituality and death that become Basheer's feminine concerns.

As a male, Basheer initially seems fixated with the body, desire and eroticism, which gradually give way to a more profound awareness about freedom and its relationship to transcendence. Narayani is linked to Basheer's more introspective, reflective self, which steers him away from the quotidian, from loneliness and sexual yearning. It makes him ponder life's deeper questions and realities and eventually leads him to a fuller awareness of who he is and what his place is in the scheme of things. It could even be argued that the source of Basheer's creativity lies in this feminine self. The woman within—Narayani—is also his muse. Basheer had to discover this self and assimilate it to achieve wholeness and, finally, inner liberation.

Predictably, after Narayani materializes, Basheer drops his elaborate plan of escaping from jail. Meanwhile, another prisoner—apparently his alter ego—who sought to flee in exactly the same manner is caught and severely beaten. The warder, who relates the story of the attempt, wonders why anyone would choose to escape when "it's better inside." Basheer not only agrees but condemns all forms of jailbreak as immoral. Since the prison is within, any real breakout must occur there. If that does not happen, the unlucky man is doomed to spend his whole life on the run. As the warder implies, physical freedom does not amount to true liberty unless one escapes from the jail within. The freedom fighter has learned what it means to be truly free.

The Question of Remembrance

Fundamental to *Mathilukal* is the issue of how Narayani will eventually be remembered. In fact, she asks Basheer this very question—whether he will remember her if she were to die. This is the first reference to death in their conversation, and, significantly, it is right after Basheer has declared that he will cover her with kisses when they meet at the hospital. Instead of reciprocating with a similar avowal of sexual love, she changes the subject. Earlier, she had spoken of the body in pain—referring to how the women in the jail had counted the 36 whiplashes inflicted on the prisoner and vicariously identified with his terrible suffering. Now, she alludes to death and memory, the extinction of body and desire, and what she will become outside her corporeal frame. Suddenly, the earlier erotic exuberance is replaced by a somber meditation on pain and dissolution and on the nature of remembrance.

The paradox at the heart of Narayani's existence is once again invoked. As body imagined, unseen and intangible, she is not unlike the presence that her memory will evoke. And yet, at the same time, she is intensely real for Basheer. How, then, must he reconcile these dualities? Basheer's rather glib reply that he will never forget her does not satisfy Narayani. She wonders how he will remember her when he has not even seen or touched her. It is a profound question that addresses the very foundations of her existence in the real world. She therefore makes Basheer reflect more deeply until he blurts out, "Your sign is all over the world. It's the truth. The walls ... Look these walls go round and round the world ..." Narayani is thus transformed into a universal and timeless symbol of freedom that transcends all walls and all prisons, including the metaphoric jail we all occupy on this earth. Removed from the personal and placed in the symbolic, she acquires the power to endure beyond the finite limits of flesh or language. She is no longer linked to either category.

Narayani's final appearance in the film is linked to the sign with which she identified herself. Before this happens, the order for Basheer's release arrives. He is now "ripe" and can go, thanks to her mediation, but how can he leave the place that has ceased to be a prison for him? When the jailer gives him the good news, he exclaims impatiently, "Why should I be free? Who wants freedom?" The materiality of freedom has no relevance for a man who has found freedom within. The only thing that matters is the prospect of losing Narayani, and he is willing to live within the walls for her sake. Basheer's final rejoinder to the jailer is that outside the prison, there is an even bigger jail. This alludes to colonial India as well as conjures up the existential metaphor of a world encircled by walls. Since one can never be free from these walls, physical freedom is no longer an issue. With his newfound vision of liberty, Basheer will be able to transcend this bigger prison.

As Basheer gets ready to leave jail in the company of the jailer, we see Narayani's sign—her branch rising and falling, outlined against the blue sky. But Basheer is unable to respond. The shot blurs as his eyes turn moist. The tears are both for Narayani, the woman he loves, and for the woman who has set him free. While parting is painful, Basheer knows that she will remain with him as a symbol of freedom's transformative power and its inherent sense of transcendence.

What is left for Basheer to do is to engage with his experience in the context of art-making. We have seen him writing before and after Narayani's advent, and when it is time for him to leave, we discover that he has been working on a manuscript entitled *Love Letter*. His encounter with Narayani—however intangible—is now given a concrete form and will endure in his fiction. In fact, we wonder whether we witnessed the whole Narayani episode while Basheer was in the process of writing it as a story.

During one of his chats with the jailer, Basheer described himself as "the flower garden and the flower ... also the fruit." In a way, the whole creative experience is summed up in this phrase that makes the artist inseparable from the created work. Basheer, who creates Narayani, exists within and with her.

Nizhalkkuthu: Dealing Death, Saving Lives

Nizhalkkuthu is set in 1941—before India's independence from British rule—in the princely state of Travancore. Although not strictly a two-part film like *Anantaram* and *Mathilukal*, its second half is the setting for the protagonist's transformative encounter with the imaginary. However, Kaliyappan couldn't be more different from Basheer and Ajayan. He is the official state hangman, to whom pen and paper, along with all conventional forms of creativity, are alien. And yet his most significant manifestation of otherness is associated with a creative act.

The premise of the film is relatively simple. The old, infirm and alcoholic Kaliyappan lives with his wife, son, Muthu, and daughter, Mallika (Figure 18). He suffers from a terrible guilt because of the innocent men he has hanged in the past. Faced with a crisis of conscience, he pleads to be let off from carrying out one last execution. But the king's decree cannot be overturned, and he reluctantly leaves his village with his son. The second half of the film focuses mostly on the events that occur on the night before the hanging when, as per custom, Kaliyappan is kept awake by the jail officials, who supply him with booze and swap stories. It is in this prison setting that the hangman will have a profound experience in which, once again, the real and the imaginary will fuse almost inextricably.

Kaliyappan's status as outsider has been determined by the state. In fact, it is integral to his appointment as official hangman. The state even demands that he stay away from its urban center and has arranged for him to live in a border village that straddles modern-day Kerala and Tamil Nadu and is accessible only by bullock cart. Physically dislocated, he stays in the margins, waiting to be summoned whenever a man is sentenced to die. The fact that he is a Tamil who lives in a Malayali village (where Malayalam is the spoken language) also stems from a decree that requires that the hangman belong to a different ethnic group. As compensation for his state-designated otherness, he is provided with a generous allowance and monetary benefits. He is also given a plot of farmland that is not taxable.

At first, the state's injunctions seem partly motivated by the fact that Kaliyappan is a dealer in death, whose profession sets him apart from others. In the popular imagination, such hangmen often become the fearsome personification of death. But there is also a larger political motive to place the man at a distance: to keep him ignorant of the legal proceedings that generate the death penalty. As hangman, his job is to carry out the state's decree, not question the verdict or feel any kind of personal responsibility for the deed. As we will see, this becomes a key issue in a state with a corrupt judiciary.

In *Nizhalkkuthu*, the state is portrayed as a highly repressive and coercive mechanism. There is virtually no scope for subjective choices, for stepping outside the rigid codes and rituals that govern almost every aspect of human behavior. It is a feudal world that exists outside time and history, its people trapped in a relentless cycle of recurrence. In fact, the sense of inevitability is so pervasive that it is accepted without question as a fact of existence. Kaliyappan's identity as the Other is constituted by and exists within this paradigm. As a creation of the state, he must live exclusively on its terms.

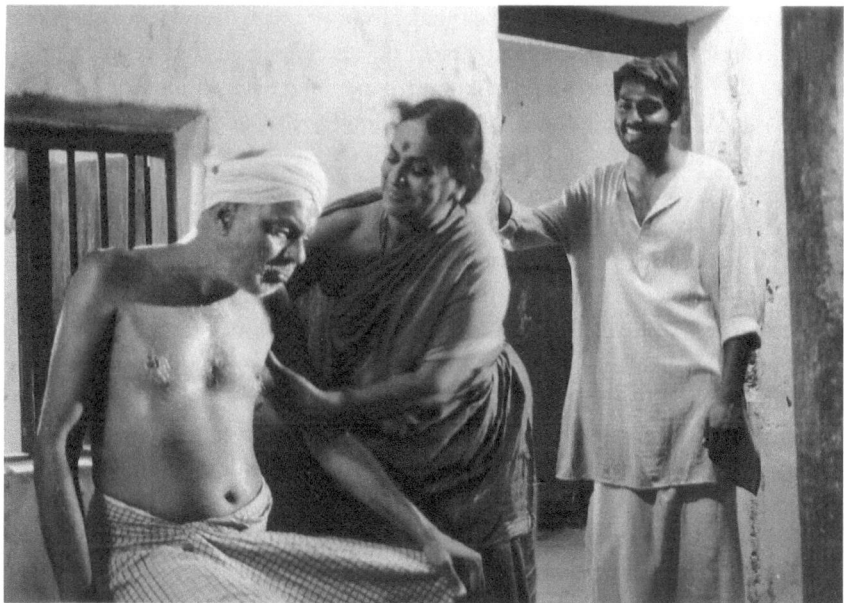

Fig. 18. *Nizhalkkuthu*. The drunk Kaliyappan with his wife and son.

The Cycle of Recurrence

Shortly after the film starts, a dissolute landlord scoffs, "Gandhi will bring us freedom!" His mockery stems from his absolute conviction that the system that has made his class a privileged species is impervious to the inroads of modernity. We know history will prove him wrong, and yet the man could be right in a way. As Gopalakrishnan has shown, despite path-breaking judicial reforms in Kerala, feudalism remains alive and well in many aspects of public life.

We learn from the same landlord that "money and influence" can buy anything these days. Justice is a travesty—the poor end up in the gallows while the guilty get off scot-free. Rather than take a stand against such blatant perversion of the law, the king of Travancore has devised a way of evading responsibility. Whenever a man is sentenced to die, he issues an unconditional pardon. However, he makes sure that it arrives as soon as the execution is over. Thus the hanging takes place on schedule while the king manages to absolve his conscience from guilt. There has never been an exception to this rule.

The king's action only confirms the idea of recurrence that Gopalakrishnan reinforces through his multiple references to rituals. When Kaliyappan's daughter attains womanhood, the timeless nature of the ceremony that marks this event is emphasized. Later, when the royal peon arrives in the village to summon Kaliyappan to the execution, his walk is photographed in long shot with a tracking camera to suggest this too is a public ritual. However much the two rites may differ in nature, they point to the larger theme of how lives are regulated by preordained patterns and how they are duplicated from generation to generation.

Although we learn that Gandhi's followers are active in Travancore, they are conspicuously absent from the film. The only Gandhian we get to know is the *charka*-spinning[4] Muthu. According to the cyclical scheme of things, he must inherit his father's profession, but the son has broken free by embracing Gandhi's creed of nonviolence. He does not eat meat, nor does he drink, and he is strongly opposed to capital punishment. Thus he stands at the extreme opposite of his hard-drinking executioner father. The elders of the village, like the landlord, brand him an "upstart" for rejecting the law of the state as well as that of the father. In their eyes, he is the Gandhian Other. His otherness is defined by his ideological commitment.

In case we pin our hopes too much on Muthu as a symbol of emancipation, Gopalakrishnan turns on a warning light quite early. There is an extraordinary cut from Muthu inserting thread into the *charka* to the rope for the hanging that is being spun in the jail by the convicts. As we watch the death rope grow in length, Muthu's thread appears tiny, almost minuscule in comparison—a portent of things to come.

Gopalakrishnan, then, gives us a father and son who approach the problem of identity in very different ways. While Muthu consciously seeks to redefine himself through a form of political activism that aims at changing the system, Kaliyappan seems locked into his professional role as hangman, destined to live and die as the state-invented Other. Meek and compliant, he is no rebel with a cause. While the son speaks out at rallies, the father does not even know how to formulate such rhetoric. Even if he knew, he probably would not dare open his mouth.

Gopalakrishnan shows how such a passive man trapped within a fixed public persona can remake himself from within. Kaliyappan may seem powerless to bend the rules that govern his professional life, but he can define himself internally, on his own terms, as the Other. Such manifestations of otherness are first placed in the contexts of faith and conscience and then linked to a creative act that catches even Kaliyappan by surprise. Each time, he successfully challenges the state's attempt to define him within its predetermined parameters.

Forms of Otherness

In the film's opening sequence, Kaliyappan sits in the local liquor den and speaks of his guilt. However much he tries to drown himself in alcohol, there is no respite from his sense of remorse. He is especially affected by the memory of a victim who had indeed committed no crime. The man had even insisted that he was innocent when Kaliyappan placed the noose around his neck, but the latter, of course, was powerless to stop the execution. He is thus almost paranoid with fear that he will be called upon to hang another such man. In a subsequent scene, he holds out his hand, black with shadows and claims it is stained with sin. His feeling of responsibility is so intense that he even blames the death of his first wife—during childbirth—on the hanging.

Such strong emotions are completely at odds with Kaliyappan's official status as state executioner. Professional hangmen are neither allowed to feel any moral compunction when they carry out their orders nor expected to suffer from any pangs of regret. It does not fall on them to judge the culpability of their victims. But in a corrupt state (even the king hides behind a fake pardon) in which the executioner serves as its killer (the generous perks are a form of bribe to keep his mouth shut), the question of assuming responsibility becomes crucial. This is precisely what Kaliyappan does. As a remorseful hangman, he becomes an anomaly. He stands apart from those around him who refuse to acknowledge their sense of complicity in the deaths. His otherness lies in this ability to empathize with the suffering of innocent victims and experience a crisis of conscience. It is thus an otherness generated within and not imposed from the outside.

The second manifestation of Kaliyappan's otherness relates to his reputation as a faith healer. He is a devotee of Kali, and all his prayers to her are accompanied by the ritual burning of a piece of rope that has been used for a hanging. When he sprinkles the ashes on the sick, they are cured almost immediately. Kaliyappan, it turns out, can perform miracles.

The first time we see him in this new role is right after he drunkenly speaks of his hands being stained with sin. The two scenes are juxtaposed to underline the paradox that is central to his existence. The man who takes away life is also responsible for saving lives. In this respect, Kaliyappan acquires a godlike stature; he bestows life and also claims it. Although he never sees himself in such terms, he is deeply aware of his double identity as executioner and healer, and he attributes this—along with everything else he accomplishes—to the goddess. Characteristically, he shirks any display of pride or ego.

Gopalakrishnan shows how such a frail and submissive man transforms himself physically and spiritually through a mysterious and intangible process that defies reason. Every time the hangman sits down to pray, we see him alone, carving out a place for himself where he communes with Kali before a shrine on which her image is kept. As he enters into the space of the ritual, he repeatedly invokes the goddess and her many attributes, surrendering his will and inviting her to make him her instrument. In this self-enclosed space, we see him achieve freedom and power that would be impossible within the constraints of his professional life.

This is dramatically borne out, especially on one occasion when after completing his ritual, Kaliyappan steps out onto the porch of his house where a sick woman lies unconscious, foaming at the mouth. With a strong gesture of his arm, he sprinkles ashes on her and then, in a loud voice, commands the evil spirit that has apparently possessed her to leave. The woman immediately rises to her feet. Thus we see the hangman recreate himself through the strength of his faith. He can forge a self, an otherness that belongs uniquely to him and that the state cannot comprehend, control or coerce. The man who defers to the state as its executioner is completely independent within his space of the healer, functioning entirely on his own terms as the Other.

The Other Eye

The final manifestation of Kaliyappan's otherness occurs in the jail, on the night before the hanging. As the jail warden and his cohorts make him drink, one of the men asks for a "spicy" story. The warden obliges with the tale of a 13-year-old-girl's rape and murder, but Gopalakrishnan chooses not to narrate the story from his perspective. Instead we see it unfold through Kaliyappan's eyes as he shapes it with his personal vision. We are, as it were, placed inside the hangman's head, where we become privy to the images that appear on his mindscreen as he applies the story directly to his own life. What begins as a fantasy or dream soon acquires a compelling reality of its own.

Empathy, as a concept, is central to *Nizhalkkuthu*. Early in the film, Kaliyappan's daughter Mallika listens to her schoolteacher recite from a book on the subject of sharing pain. He ends with a moral that defines her father's credo: "It is only when you make the pain of others your own that you become human." Kaliyappan has already proven this to be true; now he empathizes with the protagonists of a tragic tale that is about the destruction of innocence, a subject very close to his heart. Such is his degree of empathy that he literally makes these characters his own by having his family members take their place. In other words, he lives out the story, replacing the fictional characters with those who are closest to him.

At first, the warden's tale comes across as a pastoral love story replete with the usual clichés. It begins as an idyll about a village girl who grazes her goats in the forest. She is the proverbial child of nature, innocent and beautiful. When she meets a young man, his passionate flute music cuts right to her heart. They subsequently fall in love. Within this prelapsarian, Edenic world, nature is presented in all its iridescent otherness. The camera repeatedly frames the couple in relation to land, water and sky, all of which are suffused with an ethereal light. Since the girl occupies the center of this earthly paradise, she seems blissfully unaware of the perils that lurk around her. She dreams of living like a fish in the river until her lover teaches her a vital lesson about how big fish prey on small fish. He claims this is the truth that she must learn.

The serpent in this Eden turns out to be a middle-aged man who spies on the girl and makes her the object of his lustful gaze. He is not just anybody but the husband of her sister—her brother-in-law. We watch his obsession with her reach a stage where he can no longer sleep, eat or plow his fields. When he finds her alone one day, he rapes and kills her. The body is discovered and, of course, the flute player is charged with the crime. The girl's father subsequently stumbles on the truth but chooses to let it go. As the warden explains, having lost his child, he does not want his other daughter to become a widow. Thus the innocent flute player is framed as the murderer.

In Kaliyappan's transformative version, the girl becomes his own daughter, Mallika, while her ravisher and murderer is his son-in-law, Vasu. The locale is his own village, and the surrounding countryside, which we see in the main narrative, figures prominently in this story-within-a-story. Although none of the events in the warden's story have any basis in his life, they appear to be real. While the potential for such a scenario manifesting itself is slim, the possibility does exist. In short, given the quirks of human nature, it *could* happen. The hangman can sense this intuitively, and his macabre fixation with the story compels him to imagine his daughter's rape and murder.

Gopalakrishnan expects us to empathize with the events just as Kaliyappan does. Accordingly, he makes us identify closely with his point of view. Such is the intensity of the hangman's vision that soon we too seem to blur the line between the real and the imaginary. Although Gopalakrishnan disrupts the narrative twice, bringing us back to the room in the jail, we willingly suspend our disbelief and accept the facts as taking place in real time. And we accept the transposition of identities, seeing the girl as Mallika and the brother-in-law as Vasu. The fiction becomes so emphatically real that we lose our sense of bearing; there no longer seems to be a clear separation between dream and reality. Such confounding of boundaries only affirms the power of Kaliyappan's retelling of the jailer's narrative. It reveals another facet of his otherness that even he was not aware of.

In this context, the film appears strongly reflexive. We are not only directly involved in the unraveling of the story but are also made to reflect on how meaning arises from the collaboration of the teller (warden), the mediator (Kaliyappan) and the viewer (us). What makes this triangular relationship even more complex is Kaliyappan's conversion. As he appropriates the warden's story, he becomes the storyteller, inventing his own narrative with the facts of the story. This, in turn, directs our attention to the film's ultimate storyteller—its very source—Gopalakrishnan himself.

The conflation of fact and fiction, dream and reality, is also reflexive because it refers to the dreamlike nature of film and its simulation of reality. The idea is obliquely present in the title of the film, which alludes to the Indian epic, *The Mahabharata*, in which the Kaurava king Duryodhana comes up with a ruse to get rid of his cousins, the Pandavas. He orders a tribal sorcerer to perform *nizhalkkuthu* (i.e., create images of the Pandavas and then ritually slay them). As the ritual is performed, the Pandavas fall dead one by one. Thus, through sorcery, the image is brought to life and takes the place of the original just as, in the cinema, the insubstantial image—magically, as it were—replicates reality.

The film's title focuses specifically on Kaliyappan's ability to turn the warden's story into a highly subjective rendition as he breathes life into the shadows and gives them a human presence that is imbued with realism. This transformation of image into reality makes him a sorcerer of sorts and links him to the notion that creativity is indeed an intangible, magical process and the artist, who conjures up reality as if out of thin air, is actually a consummate magician. It is a deeply empowering and liberating experience.

Kaliyappan's vision is, in essence, a form of closed-eye vision. He is wide awake, but what he sees is deeply subjective and internal; it is as if he is delving into a subterranean realm, peering into his unconscious with eyes that are open and closed at the same time. In effect, he stands on the border between the rational and the irrational and communes with both aspects of his self. Thus his experience is both concrete and dreamlike at first. But what he sees gradually becomes so overpoweringly real that it is more real than reality itself. In fact, it acquires the power of truth and is compelling to such an extent that it leads to his collapse.

Kaliyappan, of course, is far from being a creative artist, but here in jail, he almost turns into one. His gift for empathy enables him to recreate and narrate the story on his own terms. In the process, as we have seen, he becomes both listener and storyteller at the same time. Here too—as in the space of his rituals—he is completely free, molding the narrative with the intensity of his vision. It is in these contexts, then, that we must appreciate this creative aspect of the hangman's self-created otherness.

The Son, the Father and the State

As the tale draws to an end, a visibly agitated Kaliyappan demands to know what befell the flute-player. He is told that he was sentenced to die. In fact, he is the innocent man Kaliyappan will hang in the morning. This is the last straw for the old man because his deepest fear seems about to materialize. His face contorted with pain, he clutches his chest and collapses. He does not die but clearly is in no state to carry out the execution the next day. Thus he escapes his fate, right under the nose of the state—a liberty due almost wholly to the power of his "other" vision. But there is a caveat. What Kaliyappan achieves must be also judged in relation to what befalls his son, which is what the film now addresses.

When Kaliyappan collapses, the state asks Muthu to carry out the abhorrent task the next morning. The latter has accompanied his father solely because of his infirmity; he remains, as before, vehemently opposed to capital punishment. Can he now hold onto his Gandhian ideals, or will he succumb to the law of the state as well as the law of the father (which calls on the son to stand by the father in his hour of need)? If the execution is delayed, the pardon will arrive, and that would completely subvert the farcical order of things, both for state and king. Since this is inconceivable, it falls on Muthu to compromise his integrity for the sake of a lying, corrupt system. At this moment of supreme crisis, he remains silent, acknowledging the impossibility of his situation. The Gandhian Other is thus tamed and brought into the fold, and the hanging takes place at the prescribed time. The film, then, ends with the father's assertion of his otherness, while the son is forced to compromise his own. Thus Kaliyappan's moment of empathy and the almost transcendental vision it begets is qualified by what befalls his son.

Although *Nizhalkkuthu* differs in many respects from *Mathilukal* and *Anantaram*, it shares with them the same engagement with the imaginary that acquires its own truth and logic as well as constitutes its own reality. As in the other films, Kaliyappan's fantastic vision is rendered with perfect realism so that we cannot tell the difference when it begins. All three films reconfigure otherness and the status of the outsider in relation to a certain interior space that is linked to creativity and emancipation. Of the three protagonists, it is perhaps Basheer, writer and freedom fighter, who most fully experiences liberation as a concept that teaches him to transcend the limits that have always circumscribed his life.

Chapter 8

THE DREAM OF EMANCIPATION: *KATHAPURUSHAN* AND THE TRIUMPH OF THE INDIVIDUAL

Kathapurushan (*Man of the Story*, 1995) is arguably Gopalakrishnan's most ambitious film, epic in scale, intimate in tone and covering nearly forty-five years of Kerala's history through the eyes of his protagonist, Kunjunni. He has called the film "an emotional journey through time and history"[1] to distinguish it from a socio-historical document, which it superficially resembles. Accordingly, all key historical events are kept off-screen. It is thus a personal film that draws on Gopalakrishnan's life and memories of the time, although it is not autobiographical in the strict sense of the term.

Kathapurushan begins with Kunjunni's birth and ends with the publication and subsequent banning of his first novel, *The Hard Consonants*. The film is primarily a cinematic *Bildungsroman* that charts the emotional and psychological evolution of a man and his consciousness and is framed by some of the key events that have shaped Kerala's modernity. Kunjunni belongs to an old feudal, land-owning family that is in decline as a result of the momentous reforms that have dramatically changed Kerala's political landscape. Thus we have another narrative about the vestigial life, except that its subject is not human decadence. Kunjunni is neither apathetic like Unni nor malignant like Patelar, nor does he hold himself aloof from the forces of modernity. Instead, he displays a progressive outlook that he uses to align himself with the historical forces that are transforming his home state. He is helped in this respect by his family, which practices an enlightened form of feudalism—feudalism with a human face. Thus *Kathapurushan* is Gopalakrishnan's most upbeat and optimistic film, where the dream of emancipation seems to be within our grasp. *Mukhamukham* was about the abject failure of that dream in relation to a demoralized community hopelessly stuck in time, but Kunjunni's choices enable him to move forward with time into a future that contains the potential for personal growth and meaningful action.

Kunjunni enters the world precariously. As a result of a breach delivery, he has to be held upside down and smacked to make him take his first breath and cry out. Later in life, he develops a stutter and a limp. Along with these markers of otherness, which point to his physical and emotional frailty, he must live with the social stigma of having been abandoned by his father. He is thus not the prototypical feudal landlord or a heroic figure but an ordinary, flawed human being whose private destiny is linked to the social and historical processes shaping Kerala as well as India as a nation. He is the *Man of the Story*—as per the film's English title—who will step outside his own class, author his life and find the common humanity he shares with everybody.

Kathapurushan begins in 1937 and covers the following: the assassination of Gandhi in 1948, the Communist electoral revolution of 1957, the Land Reforms Bill of 1959, the Naxalite uprising of 1968 and Indira Gandhi's declaration of the Emergency in 1975. These events define the contexts of Kunjunni's evolution and the reciprocal nature of his relationship to them. As he interacts and struggles with the forces unleashed by history, he is molded by them, just as he molds them to a certain extent.

Disillusioned with most forms of collective action, Gopalakrishnan once again invests in the individual. As he remarks, "In India today our crisis is due to the failure of collective action. The corruption of the collective is the crisis we face now."[2] Accordingly, he has endorsed the individual-turned-activist, who asks the right questions and mobilizes people for change, as the only source of hope. But he is realistic enough to admit that it cannot be done by just one person. As he explains, "You need several individuals, but one man can inspire others ... That has kept humanity going."[3] In *Mukhamukham*, Sudhakaran voices this sentiment after his expulsion from the Party, when he speaks of like-minded men who will bond with him to fight injustice.

For Gopalakrishnan, history is a set of variations on a theme—a series of interrogations, conflicts, transformations and refinements through which society and humanity evolve. It is an ongoing process with no pause and no promise of a utopia. The individual, by virtue of his or her actions, is an integral part of this process and, in turn, is shaped by the forces he or she sets in motion. There is thus a continuous struggle to define oneself in relation to the state and its ideology. According to Gopalakrishnan, it is one's moral duty to oppose all systems once they become inevitably rigid and oppressive. As he observes, "Any system ... soon begins to develop its own mechanisms of defenses ... It tries to annihilate individual dissent. Human progress has been mainly there because individuals have kept fighting that kind of encrustation."[4]

For Gopalakrishnan, the youthful, high-minded Kunjunni becomes the prototype of such an individual who is locked into history but can also influence the course of events through his deeply felt actions. In *Kathapurushan*, we see him pit himself against dehumanizing, repressive ideologies that are inimical to the rights and freedoms of the individual and that stand in the way of political and social justice. In the process, he has to switch camps and even oppose systems he once endorsed in order to forge new ones. Thus the fight goes on, and it enables the shy and timid Kunjunni to become the strong, independent-minded person who can be an active agent in the making of history.

The film's first half chronicles young Kunjunni's emerging consciousness of his feudal surroundings, his place in it and the gradual erosion of a way of life that dislocates him into a new era. We watch him encounter the social and political realities of this world: its power structures, inequalities and marginalized groups. The second half is about how he translates this burgeoning awareness into concrete action through the choices he makes—choices that define, among other things, his modernity of thought and purpose. The film, in fact, celebrates his ability to reject the old hierarchies and cross over to the other side, where he can create significant relationships with his social "inferiors." Underlying *Kathapurushan*, then, is a vision of enlightened self-making linked to progressive thinking that offers hope of liberation from the strictures of cyclical history.

Gopalakrishnan begins *Kathapurushan* with a prologue featuring an oral storyteller who narrates a fable. A prince and his family encounter a cannibal demon in a forest. The demon threatens to devour them all but relents; he will spare the prince and his wife in exchange for their son. The father refuses to compromise and rushes in to fight. The film starts at this point and then returns to the storyteller before the end credits. The demon now makes another deal: claiming to be invincible, he is willing to accept the wife instead of the son. But the prince defiantly brandishes his sword and reminds the demon that his victory is by no means assured. The film ends as they engage in combat.

The framing device provides *Kathapurushan* with an underlying mythic structure, the main premise of which is Kunjunni's uncompromising battle against all his adversaries. He never wavers or gives up hope of winning the war. Although the events unravel within historical time, they also acquire, by virtue of the fable, a timeless and universal dimension. The film is thus, in terms of form, a complex mix of the personal, historical and mythic, all of which coexist and complement one another.

Spaces of the Other

The ancestral home in which Kunjunni grows up is run by his highly capable grandmother, who is also an enlightened matriarch with a benevolent side. The other woman in the house is Kunjunni's mother, an elusive figure who suffers from a chronic ailment that keeps her in bed most of the time. Abandoned by her husband—he left her for another woman—her illness reflects her inner grieving. Ailing and sad-faced, she is always shot in relation not only to her bed but to doorways and barred windows: liminal spaces (Figure 19).

Fig. 19. *Kathapurushan*. The infant Kunjunni in his mother's arms.

The two servants—Veluchar and Janamma—have been with the family for years. While Veluchar is single, Janamma is married to the weak and ineffectual Pachupillai. They have several children, the eldest being Meenakshi, who is about Kunjunni's age.

Even as a young boy, Kunjunni is conscious of the hierarchies into which he has been born, addressed and deferred to as *yajamanan* (master) by the servants, who are obviously much older than him. It is through his close proximity to the Other that he discovers the plain and simple truth that the world is riven by social and economic disparities. Although they all live under the same roof, these Others clearly do not subscribe to his sense of home and class. Their presence underlines an unequal feudal structure of wealth and privilege.

His friendship with Meenakshi gives Kunjunni access to her dysfunctional family, which is scarred by deprivation, poverty and internal discord. The father—Pachupillai—often stays away from home, does odd jobs, squanders his wages on drink and has extra-marital affairs while saddling his wife with children they can ill afford. His frequent desertions and his disdain for his commitments as husband and father are the source of an ongoing crisis. Their day-to-day subsistence is so fraught with peril that without the support and generosity of Kunjunni's grandmother, they would be out in the street.

Kunjunni watches Pachupillai eat greedily "like an elephant" (as the latter claims). Nobody eats like that in his home. When his uncle Vasu, a freedom-fighter on the run, suddenly appears with a three-day-hunger, we see him eat decorously from a banana leaf, not once betraying his famished condition. But Pachupillai eats like a man possessed—another marker of difference. Food, devoured with such physical urgency, becomes a new and coveted object in the boy's eyes.

The wife—Janamma—is physically large and corpulent, with great reserves of energy. Unlike Kunjunni's depressed, mostly bedridden mother, this laborer woman works vigorously all day. She comes across as tough and feisty, railing at her husband for flouting his responsibilities. He rarely retaliates, clearly intimidated by her. At the same time, the two remain close, sexually and otherwise.

Everything Kunjunni experiences during his visits seems completely at odds with his sense of his family as a self-contained, stable unit built on the bedrock of tradition and ritual. But he too has a father who has shunned his duties and is absent from their lives, and his mother's illness is a reminder of her profound unhappiness. Despite these parallels, the fact remains that the two families belong to different worlds.

If Kunjunni had remained an aloof outsider looking in with a detached, critical gaze, he would have doubtlessly thought himself entitled and superior in relation to Meenakshi's family. But his close ties with her and his regular visits make him an integral part of her milieu. Throughout his childhood, his gaze is open and curious. Thus he does not simply turn away from what is initially baffling and subversive in relation to his notion of home and family. He registers the difference but does not reject it as perverse.

Kunjunni learns about difference in spatial terms as well. Meenakshi and her family live in a part of the house that is reserved for servants. Veluchar has his place there, too. Domestic space is thus divided along lines of class and labor. Kunjunni can grasp this intuitively because he moves between his space and their space. This fluid movement between separate realms enables him to stay within and yet stand outside the hierarchy that governs the divisions within the household. He is aware of the demarcations of his space, but he also knows he can easily transcend them.

Thanks to the remarkable liberal outlook of his grandmother, there has never been a rigid mapping of social spaces within the house. As an authority figure, she exercises power firmly but fairly. She treats the servants humanely, as if they were an extension of the family, and they, in turn, reciprocate with warmth and feeling. When Janamma and her family leave for good, the grandmother gives her own gold necklace to Meenakshi for her marriage. Thus the lines separating employer and employee remain fluid at all times, but this does not lead to their erasure. The servants are grateful for the kindness and respect shown to them but, at the same time, are fully aware of their place within the social setup. Kunjunni will inherit his grandmother's combination of strength and gentleness and her large-hearted humanism. He will also take her liberalism much further than she could have imagined by marrying Meenakshi.

Gopalakrishnan shows how children are natural transgressors of the boundaries adults create. Just as Kunjunni effortlessly crosses into her social space, Meenakshi moves fluidly into his. As his playmate and occasional tormentor (she likes to tease and frighten him), she grows up virtually within his household (she learns to read with help from Kunjunni's mother) (Figure 20). However, this does not stop her from addressing him as *yajamanan*. Even at that young age, she is conscious of her liminal status, made to feel at home and yet never quite at home. She is very conscious of this ambivalence, treated as an equal by Kunjunni, yet aware of her social and economic marginalization. (She is given free meals that are daily acts of charity.) At the end of each day, she knows she must vacate his space and cross over to the other side—her side.

If the crippling power of the word *yajamanan* seems impossible to ignore, Gopalakrishnan offers a wonderful liberating moment in the film during which the two children free themselves from the social and ideological baggage of language. Meenakshi wakes up Kunjunni in the morning and badgers him to play with her. He protests, she cries, he makes up—it is all done through sounds, via the consonants each utters (Kunjunni, of course, stutters). Although done in play, they invent their own language that rejects the one they have been taught to speak and defines them as server and served.

Along with Meenakshi, Kunjunni's other guide to alien social spaces is the older Veluchar, who keeps an eye on him at all times. His relationship with this middle-aged servant is more complex because the latter becomes, in effect, his surrogate father. Veluchar takes him to school, disciplines him when necessary, talks to him about a variety of things and takes good care of him (while, of course, addressing him as *yajamanan*). Kunjunni even goes to his room to sleep at night when he feels insecure, thus crossing a major spatial and social divide. It is significant that, on one such occasion, he asks Veluchar about the absence of his biological father. Along with the reconfiguration of space, Kunjunni and Veluchar's closeness also points to a significant reframing of roles and identities.

For Kunjunni, Veluchar is an interesting example of a crossover who falls outside the categories of *them* and *us*. As the retainer of a feudal family, he identifies so completely with its rituals and traditions that any slur directed at it is unacceptable. In other words, he has crossed over to their side while remaining a servant. He is strongly anti-Gandhi and anti-reform and reacts angrily to the Land Reforms Bill that will end the family's monopoly as landowners. He even criticizes a low-caste teacher

Fig. 20. *Kathapurushan*. Kunjunni and Meenakshi as children.

who would not take his shoes off while walking past their house. It would be easy to dismiss Veluchar as hopelessly colonized by the system he works for, but for Gopalakrishnan, he is simply like any other man: full of quirks, inconsistencies and contradictions.

The Absent Father

Shortly after Kunjunni's birth, the astrologer arrives to predict his future. When the mother falls ill, an *ayurvedic* physician recites a list of medicines based on ancient texts. At night, the grandmother reads to her grandson from the sacred books. Kunjunni grows up within established patterns of living that have remained unchanged for generations. What is not quite right is his father's conspicuous absence.

In a film that endorses modernity, Gopalakrishnan is careful not to dismiss the astrologer as a symbol of a worn-out orthodoxy. In fact, all his predictions turn out to be true. The system—however unscientific—has its own logic and place within the larger scheme of things and makes perfect sense in such a context. There is thus no glib attempt to place progress above and against tradition (unless the latter is deemed oppressive). More important for Gopalakrishnan is to define those elements that are integral to a particular way of life and make that life what it is. In fact, the old and the new are not shown to be antithetical but rather complementary. In the scene featuring the *ayurvedic* physician, Kunjunni is shown fiddling with a bicycle. There is no contrived attempt here to emphasize it as a symbol of technology. Instead, the two coexist without any apparent disharmony. The scene closes with the physician joking about how Kunjunni will scrape his shins if he tries to ride the bicycle. There is a tacit assumption that one day the boy will indeed learn to bike, but that will not contradict or challenge what the physician stands for and practices.

Perhaps the most prominent symbol of modernity and change in the first half is M. K. Gandhi, who spells doom for Kunjunni's feudal universe. The boy is too young to understand what the man actually represents, but he can sense his symbolic presence in his life. When uncle Vasu shows up one night after a long absence, hounded by the police, Kunjunni hears him talk about Gandhi's movement for independence, which is close to fruition. Vasu, who started out as a Gandhian and has now embraced communism to bring about the "complete" revolution, provides Kunjunni with his first glimpse into the arcane world of politics. His unkempt, bearded visage and the fact that he is on the run and wanted for murder (among other crimes) make him a fascinating, exotic creature. Kunjunni's adoption of political radicalism as a young man may have its indirect source in Vasu. Like his uncle, he too will rebel against his own class and its ideology, but his commitment will be much stronger than Vasu's.

At the news of Gandhi's assassination, Kunjunni bursts into tears. He watches the local Congress workers file past in a silent procession to honor the man venerated as Father of the Nation. The tears may seem strange until we place them in the context of his own father's absence, which he keenly feels because of the social stigma attached to it (when the *ayurvedic* physician inquires about the man, there is a cut to Kunjunni lowering his eyes) and that translates into his sense of rejection. Although brought up among women in a matrilineal society, the boy is fully aware of the power and status of men. Even divinity, he discovers, is predominantly male in terms of gender (when he spends the night in Veluchar's room, the servant sings a hymn to the god Rama). And in the larger world outside, men, like Gandhi, embody paternity and make things happen. Denied his father's stabilizing presence, which would have helped him achieve both self-definition and respectability, Kunjunni has identified with the country's preeminent symbol of fatherhood and is now orphaned like the rest of the nation. It is his first encounter with the symbolic—in political terms—and anticipates his subsequent immersion in public life as an activist. As for now, Kunjunni struggles to overcome his sense of loss by rubbing bear fat above his lip. The hope is that it will sprout a moustache and thus accelerate his growth toward the comforting security of manhood.

It needs to be pointed out here that, with a few exceptions, virtually all the males in the first half (and, for that matter, the rest of the film) prove to be ineffectual, a fact Kunjunni registers because of his extreme sensitivity to this issue. Both his father and Pachupillai are guilty of desertion. The eccentric Vasu, in his own way, is guilty of the same, having left the family to study in England (which entailed selling off acres of prime land to pay for his passage fare). It all came to nothing when he returned home and decided to join Gandhi. At both times, his presence at home was needed. When he reappears in the second half, it is as an ascetic who has abandoned his political life along with his wife and children (who can barely subsist on what he has left them). The failure of all three men as husbands and fathers is placed within the self-indulgent, enervating culture of feudalism. It is women who almost always pay the price, as Kunjunni discovers, watching his mother pine away and die prematurely.

It is her death that occasions Kunjunni's father's only appearance in the film. He alights from his car as his son, who has been summoned from his college hostel, is preparing to light the funeral pyre. We see him from Kunjunni's perspective as an affluent middle-aged man who remains a stranger in the crowd, as he is to his son. It is significant that the two meet in the context of death—a death for which the latter is largely responsible. There is no exchange of words, no display of contrition or forgiveness. In fact, the father can barely meet his son's gaze. He will remain dead to the son until the end of the film, when a man who claims to be Kunjunni's half brother informs him that their father is mortally ill and would like to see him. Thus it is the imminence of death that creates the possibility of their reunion. However, the bitter Kunjunni is reluctant to oblige, claiming that a father's role does not begin and end with procreation. But his own son urges him to change his mind, reminding him that one day he too will be old and infirm. It is thus a son's voice from another time and another generation that makes a father reconsider his decision. By the time Kunjunni gets there, the man is dead.

This small but significant scene is played out in relation to the life Kunjunni has created for his own family, where there is mutual love, respect and caring. They live quite happily together without having to worry about power games or any form of hierarchy (they have no servants). We can feel their contentment as they indulge in the simple joy of watering plants in their garden in a discord-free familial space. The fact that Kunjunni could not be at his dying father's bedside is no longer an issue. It is the reality of their present, with its sense of harmony and fulfillment, that makes up amply for the disappointments of the past.

Generally, it is from the father that the male child learns about authority and power. But in his absence and in a matrilineal culture, Kunjunni's model is his grandmother. Calm and poised at all times, she never once has to raise her voice to assert herself; her presence alone enforces obedience. Kunjunni's experience of authority outside this self-contained world is inevitably dislocating. In fact, he is scarred by his very first encounter.

Learning the hard consonants at his preschool is challenging enough, but especially so for the five-year-old Kunjunni who is easily distracted by the antics of a goat feeding on the leaves of a plant. When the scowling teacher (who addresses him as *yajamanan*) demands that he utter the sounds, the terrified Kunjunni acquires a painful stutter. It will persist for a good part of his life and will set him apart from others. It will be a sign, in fact, of his vulnerability that he will overcome largely through his political activism.

With regard to authority figures, Kunjunni also discovers that outside home, his privileged status as *yajamanan* cannot shield him. In fact, he finds out—a few years later—that it can actually work against him when his low-caste teacher puts him down as "a petit bourgeois". Kunjunni does not comprehend the meaning of the term, and his family cannot help him. Alien and exotic, it is dismissed as an obscene word by Veluchar. Nobody catches the subtle premonition that the world is changing and that "upstart" teachers are no longer willing to defer to the authority of a fading and decadent system.

Purging the Feudal Within

There is a direct cut from Kunjunni experimenting with bear fat to Kunjunni as a young man (with his stutter intact) living in his college hostel. It is as if his wish to become an adult has been magically fulfilled. Almost ten years elapse via this abrupt transition, and it prepares us for similar ellipses in this final section of the film. The sudden temporal disjunction begs a crucial question: has Kunjunni finally freed himself from the stranglehold of his regressive feudal time, as the jump cut seems to suggest? The question is indirectly broached by one of his college friends, who claims that Kunjunni remains a diehard feudal inside. We see the latter lower his eyes as if tacitly acknowledging the charge.

The second half of *Kathapurushan* could be seen as Kunjunni's struggle to expunge the lingering residue of his feudal consciousness. By participating in virtually all the key historical and political movements of his time, he strives to prove that he can turn his back on his class and its ideology and become an outsider to his own legacy and inheritance. Thus a psychological compulsion underlies his choices as an ardent political activist.

Although the film glosses over the Communist electoral victory of 1957, we can assume that Kunjunni, who was 20 at the time, was involved in the process that led to this extraordinary event. We see him support the historic Land Reforms Act of 1959, which would end the power of the feudal landlords and give away land to the peasants. As a result of such legislation, Kunjunni's family is reduced to poverty. Even before the bill is passed, we learn that the lessees have stopped giving the family their dues. When Veluchar bemoans the passage of the bill, Kunjunni voices his newfound political faith by claiming that the land belongs to the tiller. When Veluchar retorts that he talks just like a communist, Kunjunni offers only an enigmatic smile.

The hardships that follow are vividly documented. Meenakshi's family is sent away because it is no longer possible to afford servants. The few acres that are left have to be pawned to pay for Kunjunni's college tuition. But the human cost does not deter his endorsement of the bill because the interests of the Party must come before those of his family and himself. Kunjunni is glad to affirm that he's a "bad" feudal, or, even better, an enemy of his class.

In 1968, when the Naxalites, a Maoist group, begin their armed insurrection against landlords and moneylenders in Kerala, Kunjunni joins them and becomes one of the local leaders. Although the film does not explain why he subscribes to a radical ideology that espouses violence, it is likely that Kunjunni was deeply disillusioned by the breakup of the Communist Party in 1964 and sought an alternative to it.

Arrested for publishing clandestine literature, Kunjunni is tortured in jail. This leaves him with a limp. This second brush with authority scars him as well—this time for life. What is profoundly ironic is the fact that Kerala, at this point in history, is under a Marxist government. Its brutal reprisals are directed at its former comrades who have dared to leave the fold. What was once a government of the people has now turned into an authoritarian and coercive establishment that is intolerant of any dissent. The portrait of Gandhi—the exponent of nonviolence—hanging on the wall of the police station is a travesty.

After his acquittal, Kunjunni becomes a writer. This is a new form of activism. The book he writes, *The Hard Consonants*, drawing on his life and times, is both personally therapeutic as well as politically "explosive" (as a reviewer brands it). Kunjunni explains that the work "could be fiction ... it could be facts." The fiction, we assume, allows him the space to invent and reinvent himself in relation to the events of his public and personal life. It provides him with the distance he needs to look back on the choices he made. The title, with its obvious allusion to his childhood trauma, affirms that he has not only mastered the consonants (and become a successful writer) but has also defeated many hard adversaries over the years and, in the process, transcended his fear and timidity. He has come through, and the book bears testament to that compelling victory.

Much of the writing is undertaken during Prime Minister Indira Gandhi's Emergency (1975–77). By then the Naxal movement had been brutally suppressed, and India was in the grip of an authoritarian regime, its democracy at stake. In such a climate of fear, the writing of Kunjunni's book is a subversive act. Its subsequent publication in Kerala coincides with the return to power of the communists—the Left Front Alliance—in 1980. The book reportedly enjoys record sales in the state and sends "shock waves in political circles." Predictably, the government bans the novel as too inflammatory. Those behind the decision are, of course, Kunjunni's old Marxist allies. It is the all-too-familiar scenario of an elected government denying people their freedom of expression and their right to disagree. This oppressor too, then, must be fought. Like the prince in the frame story, Kunjunni is resolved to take on each and every adversary who threatens basic rights and liberties. Even when victory seems elusive, the important thing is not to give up the struggle or consider the enemy unvanquishable. The prince's retort to the demon in the frame story—"What makes you think you'll always be the victor?"—applies to Kunjunni's courage, determination and refusal to compromise.

Kunjunni reacts to the news of the ban by laughing uproariously. His tells his wife (Meenakshi, whom he married on his release from jail) and son, with evident sarcasm, that the government's action only proves how much it fears the unsavory truth of his work. He must not hide or live in fear but instead battle this new enemy with his pen. As Kunjunni speaks with passion, empowered by his sense of purpose, his stutter is cured for good. In this respect, it is really his triumph, and it frees him through his laughter from precisely the forces that seek to oppress him.

Our last glimpse of Kunjunni is in the company of his wife and son, reciting the hard consonants together. Kunjunni can now rattle them off without stumbling once. We are reminded of the earlier scene between him and Meenakshi, when it was still a struggle for him to make the same sounds. His son (played by the actor who played the young Kunjunni) now recites the consonants with him. Thus, Gopalakrishnan brings together past, present and future in an eloquent vindication of the family, its solidarity and its human worth, without which all forms of activism are meaningless.

At the end of *Kathapurushan*, we are left with the all-important question of whether Kunjunni has indeed erased all traces of his feudal inheritance and truly become an outsider to his class. His activism and personal choices suggest that this could be the case. Perhaps his most radical choice has been to marry Meenakshi, thus finally dismantling the master-servant divide that governed social relations in his house for generations. He marries her for her worth as a person and as a woman and refuses to ask for a dowry. When her good-for-nothing father, in turn, asks *him* for money, he pays him the price for her liberty. Keenly aware of the plight of women in a patriarchal world since he was a boy, Kunjunni's actions are further proof of his broad-minded, modern sensibility.

Shortly after his marriage, Kunjunni sells the ancestral mansion, thus physically severing all ties with the past. He aptly compares the house to a rusty, leaking ship "abandoned in the sea, waiting for its final immersion." The new owner is a man who worked as a servant for the family many years ago and, thanks to his nouveau riche son, can now claim the property that once belonged to his *yajamanan*. As he prepares to move in, Kunjunni moves into a modest house with his wife. This reversal is a prime example of the leveling of social and economic differences that has its source in Kerala's historic reforms. But Gopalakrishnan shrewdly hints at what is ahead—the new hierarchies that burgeoning capitalism will generate. The Kunjunnis of the future will have to take their fight to a new terrain.

Gopalakrishnan has never again attempted a film like *Kathapurushan*, with its complex movement through time and its vision of emancipation that extends to almost all spheres of social and political life. In relation to his narratives of decadence and dislocation, battles lost to the forces of orthodoxy and the failure to achieve some form of personal and collective transformation, *Kathapurushan* makes the struggle seem worthwhile in terms of what it projects as a vision of the future. We see the end of feudal Kerala, the dismantling of hierarchies, Kujunni's rejection of his class and privileges and his fight as an agent of history against all forms of oppression. There could be no better endorsement of a progressive agenda shaped by the modernity of choice and outlook, and yet it all seems too good to be true, making the idealism suspect.

Like all proponents of humanist cinema, Gopalakrishnan faces the challenge of having to constantly reconfigure the grounds of his humanism in relation to a dynamic, ever-changing and unpredictable contemporaneity. As we've seen in the case of *Vidheyan*, the tendency to invest in human goodness in absolute terms or to treat the oppressor as an innocent victim of his feudal heritage puts him at risk of coming across as naïve and shortsighted. In *Kathapurushan* (and elsewhere), his cynicism about collective action and his full investment in the individual as activist may seem out of touch with the complexities of postmodern life where we are constantly reminded of the sheer scale and anonymity of the forces arrayed against us. The individual is dwarfed and rendered puny, not heroic. Gopalakrishnan's reluctance to engage with the larger contemporary realities within and outside Kerala and his immersion in the feudal past (beginning with *Nizhalkkuthu*, several of his recent films have been set in pre-independence India), may suggest a regressive tendency—a clinging to an outdated humanism that has little relevance to the world in which we live today. And yet to judge his legacy merely in terms of its contemporaneity is to do him a grave injustice. The idealism of *Kathapurushan*, however problematic for some, is based on life-affirming, real values that could be described as—to use those much-maligned terms—timeless and universal. Such idealism enables us to understand the enduring quality of Gopalakrishnan's cinema, which while embracing historical specificity also seeks to transcend it. Hence the emphasis on emancipation surpasses its political and social contexts and applies to the human condition in its totality. It would be impossible to sustain such a belief without a firm grounding in values that are neither contemporary nor retrograde but seek to define what is vital and essential to the challenge of living. *Kathapurushan*'s centrality in relation to the films that came before and after it in Gopalakrishnan's oeuvre is due to the fact that it not only reiterates the conflicts that occur in his films but also offers us a vision of transcendence that is not merely about Kunjunni's triumph. It makes us aspire to live in this world with purpose and a sense of affirmation, despite the adversarial forces that threaten to undermine such desire. It persuasively argues for the need to keep trying so that the vindication of the act of living itself becomes its most powerful emancipatory message. The film, then, functions both within and outside its historically determined contexts. It meticulously documents the ideological and social processes at work but ultimately offers us a vision that is larger than those processes. We are urged not to give up the fight but strive to exceed ourselves. The film thus lifts us out of the despair and sense of stopped time that *Mukhamukham* embodies. It seems only fitting, then, to close this study with *Kathapurushan* which, more than any other of Gopalakrishnan's films, offers us a truly liberating vision about choosing life and learning how to live it fully.

FILMOGRAPHY

Swayamvaram (***One's Own Choice,*** **1972**)
Producer:	Chitralekha Film Cooperative
Screenplay:	Adoor Gopalakrishnan
Cinematography:	Mankada Ravi Varma
Music:	M. B. Srinivasan
Cast:	Madhu, T. Sarada, Lalitha, P. K. Venukuttan Nair, Thikkurissi Sukumaran Nair
Length:	125 minutes

Kodiyettam (***The Ascent,*** **1977**)
Producer:	Chitralekha Film Cooperative
Screenplay:	Adoor Gopalakrishnan
Cinematography:	Mankada Ravi Varma
Cast:	Gopi, Vilasani, Lalitha, Adoor Bhavani, Aziz, Kaviyoor Ponnamma
Length:	128 minutes

Elippathayam (***The Rat Trap,*** **1981**)
Producer:	Ravi, General Pictures
Screenplay:	Adoor Gopalakrishnan
Cinematography:	Mankada Ravi Varma
Music:	M. B. Srinivasan
Cast:	Karamana Janardhanan Nair, T. Sarada, Jalaja, Rajam K. Nair, Joycee
Length:	121 minutes

Mukhamukham (***Face to Face,*** **1984**)
Producer:	Ravi, General Pictures
Screenplay:	Adoor Gopalakrishnan
Cinematography:	Mankada Ravi Varma
Music:	M. B. Srinivasan
Cast:	P. Ganga, Kaviyoor Ponnamma, Karamana Janardhanan Nair, Ashokan, Lalitha
Length:	107 minutes

Anantaram (***Monologue,*** **1987**)
Producer:	Ravi, General Pictures
Screenplay:	Adoor Gopalakrishnan
Cinematography:	Mankada Ravi Varma
Music:	M. B. Srinivasan
Cast:	Ashokan, Sudheesh, Mammootty, Shobana, Kaviyoor Ponnamma
Length:	125 minutes

Mathilukal (*The Walls*, 1989)
Producer: Adoor Gopalakrishnan Productions
Screenplay: Adoor Gopalakrishnan, based on a work by Vaikom Muhammad Basheer
Cinematography: Mankada Ravi Varma
Music: Vijaya Bhaskar
Cast: Mammootty, Ravi Vallathol, Thilakan, Lalitha (Narayani's voice)
Length: 117 minutes

Vidheyan (*The Servile*, 1993)
Producer: Ravi, General Pictures
Screenplay: Adoor Gopalakrishnan, based on a work by Paul Zacharia
Cinematography: Mankada Ravi Varma
Music: Vijaya Bhaskar
Cast: Mammootty, M. R. Gopakumar, Sabita Anand, Tanvi Azmi
Length: 112 minutes

Kathapurushan (*Man of the Story*, 1995)
Producer: Adoor Gopalakrishnan Productions and Japan Broadcasting Corporation
Screenplay: Adoor Gopalakrishnan,
Cinematography: Mankada Ravi Varma
Music: Vijaya Bhaskar
Cast: Viswanathan, Mini Nair, Arnamula Ponnamma, Babu Namboothiri, Lalitha, Oduvil Unnikrishnan
Length: 107 minutes

Nizhalkkuthu (*Shadow Kill*, 2002)
Producer: Adoor Gopalakrishnan Productions and Artcam International
Screenplay: Adoor Gopalakrishnan,
Cinematography: Mankada Ravi Varma and Sunny Joseph
Music: Illayaraja
Cast: Oduvil Unnikrishnan, Sunil, Reeja, Sivakumar, Murali
Length: 90 minutes

Naalu Pennungal (*Four Women*, 2007)
Producer: Adoor Gopalakrishnan
Screenplay: Adoor Gopalakrishnan, based on stories by Thakazhi Sivasankara Pillai
Cinematography: M. J. Radhakrishnan
Music: Isaac Thomas
Cast: Padmapriya, Sreejith, Geetu Mohandas, Manju Pillai, Nandita Das, Kavya Madhavan, Ravi Vallathol
Length: 105 minutes

Oru Pennum Randaanum (*A Climate for Crime*, 2008)
Producer: Adoor Gopalakrishnan
Screenplay: Adoor Gopalakrishnan, based on stories by Thakazhi Sivasankara Pillai
Cinematography: M. J. Radhakrishnan
Music: Isaac Thomas
Cast: M. R. Gopakumar, Kuttan Pillai, Vijayaraghavan, Krishnakumar, Praveena, Ravi Vallathol, Manoj K. Jayan, Jagadeesh, Sudheesh.
Length: 115 minutes

NOTES

Introduction

1. Lalit Mohan Joshi, and C. S. Venkiteswaran, eds., *A Door to Adoor* (London: South Asian Cinema Foundation, 2006).
2. Gautaman Bhaskaran, *Adoor Gopalakrishnan: A Life in Cinema* (New Delhi: Penguin India, 2010).
3. Maithili Rao. "Adoor Gopalakrishnan—The Apolitical Humanist Projects the Sky on a Dew Drop." In *A Door to Adoor*, edited by Lalit Mohan Joshi and C. S. Venkiteswaran. London: South Asian Cinema Foundation, 2006: 34–35.
4. P. K. Nair, "Some Memorable Moments in Adoor's Films." In *A Door to Adoor*, edited by Lalit Mohan Joshi and C. S. Venkiteswaran. London: South Asian Cinema Foundation, 2006: 121.
5. Muraleedharan Tharayil. "*Elippathayam: Rat Trap*." In *Cinema of India*, edited by Lalitha Gopalan, 191–199. London and New York: Wallflower Press, 2010: 195.
6. Lalit Mohan Joshi. "*Nizhalkkuthu*—The Epic Conflict." In *A Door to Adoor*, edited by Lalit Mohan Joshi and C. S. Venkiteswaran. London: South Asian Cinema Foundation, 2006:112.
7. Ella Datta. "Authority and the Individual." *Telegraph*, Calcutta, September 10, 2000: 18.
8. Ravi Vasudevan, e-mail to author, January 8, 2013.
9. Suranjan Ganguly. "Mapping Interiors: An Interview with Adoor Gopalakrishnan." *Asian Cinema* 9, no. 1 (1997): 3.
10. Saibal Chatterjee. "Master's Vision." *Outlook*, April 2, 1997: 59.
11. Aruna Vausudev. "Adoor Gopalakrishnan: Beyond the Wall." *Cinemaya* 22 (1994): 22.
12. Khalid Mohamed. "The Unseen Woman." *Times of India*, March 4, 1990: 4.
13. Ganguly, "Mapping Interiors," 8.
14. Mohamed, "Unseen Woman," 4.
15. Ganguly, "Mapping Interiors," 5.
16. Ibid., 11.
17. Bikram Singh. "Anybody Who Says It Is an Anti-Marxist Film Has Absolutely Not Understood It." *Sunday Observer*, December 2, 1984: 15.
18. Shobha Warrier. "You Want the Audience to Come and Watch Your Film on Your Terms, Not Theirs." *Sunday Observer*, July 21–27, 1996: 4.
19. C. S. Venkiteswaran. "*Swayamvaram*—Classic Prophecies." In *A Door to Adoor*, edited by Lalit Mohan Joshi and C. S. Venkiteswaran. London: South Asian Cinema Foundation, 2006: 27.
20. Ashish Rajadhyaksha. "Adoor Gopalakrishnan." In *Encyclopaedia of Indian Cinema*, edited by Ashish Rajadhyaksha and Paul Willemen. London: British Film Institute, 1994: 97.
21. Ibid.

22 Tharayil, "*Elippathayam*," 192.
23 Ibid.
24 K. Santosh. "Decades of Struggle and Surprise." *Hindu*, November 28, 1997. Accessed January 7, 2013. http://www.webpage.com/hindu/daily/971128/09
25 Adoor Gopalakrishnan. "Satyajit Ray." In *Satyajit Ray at 70*, edited by Nemai Ghosh and Alok Nandi. Hyderabad: Orient Longman, 1992: 96.
26 Rajeev Srinivasan. "The Movie Interview." *Rediff on the Net*, July 31, 1997. Accessed February 7, 2011. http://www.redifindia.com/entertai/jul31adoor.htm
27 Rajadhyaksha, "Adoor Gopalakrishnan," 97.
28 Ed Halter. "Final Destination: The God of Small Things." *Village Voice*, April 30–May 6, 2003. Accessed January 6, 2012. http://www.villagevoice.com/film/0318,halter43698,20.html
29 Bryan Walsh. "Knee Deep in the New Wave." *Time*, April 28, 2003. Accessed January 7, 2013. http://www.time.com/time/printout/0,8816,447254,00.html
30 Adoor Gopalakrishnan in conversation with the author, December 2005.
31 Italo Spinelli. "Interview with Adoor Gopalakrishnan." *Indian Summer*, Locarno Film Festival brochure, 2002. Accessed January 10, 2010. http://www.kagw.com/adoor/italo_spiineeli_interview.htm
32 Yves Thoraval. *Cinemas of India*. New Delhi: Macmillan India, 2000: 221.
33 R. Krishnakumar. "Cinema with a Purpose." *Frontline*, August 9–22, 1997. Accessed January 7, 2013. http://www.the-hindu.com/fline/fl1416/14161560.htm
34 Ibid.
35 Chatterjee, "Master's Vision," 59.
36 Ibid.
37 Warrier, "You Want the Audience," 4.
38 Sangeeta Datta. *Shyam Benegal*. London: British Film Institute, 2008: 23.
39 Ibid., 26.
40 In 2012 the Adoor Gopalakrishnan Archive and Research Fund (http://www4.uwm.edu/psoa/film/adoor-gopalakrisnan-archive.cfm) was created at the University of Wisconsin–Milwaukee, USA. It is committed, among other things, to making the films available in a digitized format.

1. Things Fall Apart: *Mukhamukham* and the Failure of the Collective

1 Adoor Gopalakrishnan. "The Director about the Film." In *Face to Face*, edited by Shampa Banerjee. Calcutta: Seagull Press, 1985: n.p.
2 Bikram Singh. "Anybody Who Says It Is an Anti-Marxist Film Has Absolutely Not Understood It." *Sunday Observer*, December 2, 1984: 15.
3 Vausudev, Aruna. "Adoor Gopalakrishnan: Beyond the Wall." *Cinemaya* 22 (1994): 19.
4 Gopalakrishnan, "Director About the Film," n. p.
5 Adoor Gopalakrishnan in conversation with the author, April 2013.

2. The Domain of the Inertia: *Elippathayam* and the Crisis of Masculinity

1 T. J. Nossiter. *Communism in Kerala*. Berkeley and Los Angeles: University of California Press, 1982: 28.

2 Ibid.
3 C.S.Venkiteswaran. "A Door to Adoor." In *A Door to Adoor*, edited by Lalit Mohan Joshi and C. S. Venkiteswaran. London: South Asian Cinema Foundation, 2006: 80.
4 Adoor Gopalakrishnan. "Adoor on Adoor Films." In *Adoor Gopalakrishnan: Twenty Five Years of Filmmaking*, edited by S. B. Jayaram. Trivandrum: Chalachithra, 1996: 36.
5 Aloknanda Datta and Soma Roy. "Adoor Gopalakrishnan in Conversation." *Splice* 2 (1986): 28.
6 Ibid., 27.
7 Gonul Donmez-Colin. "Aesthetics of Politics: Adoor Gopalakrishnan." *Deep Focus* 8, nos. 1–2 (1998): 94.

3. Master and Slave: *Vidheyan* and the Debasement of Power

1 Vausudev, Aruna. "Adoor Gopalakrishnan: Beyond the Wall." *Cinemaya* 22 (1994): 22.
2 Ibid.
3 Adoor Gopalakrishnan in conversation with the author, October 2009.
4 Vasudev, "Adoor Gopalakrishnan," 23.
5 Martine Armand. "Notes on Adoor Gopalakrishnan's Cinema." Festival de Films de Fribourg brochure (1997): 118.
6 C. S.Venkiteswaran. "A Door to Adoor." In *A Door to Adoor*, edited by Lalit Mohan Joshi and C. S. Venkiteswaran. London: South Asian Cinema Foundation, 2006: 94.

4. The Server and the Served: *Kodiyettam* and the Politics of Consumption

1 Aloknanda Datta and Soma Roy. "Adoor Gopalakrishnan in Conversation." *Splice* 2 (1986): 26.
2 Uma Da Cunha. "*Kodiyettam*." In *Film India: The New Generation, 1960–1980*, edited by Uma da Cunha. New Delhi: Directorate of Film Festivals, 1981: 87.
3 Adoor Gopalakrishnan. "Adoor on Adoor Films." In *Adoor Gopalakrishnan: Twenty Five Years of Filmmaking*, edited by S. B. Jayaram. Trivandrum: Chalachithra, 1996: 34.

6. Woman in the Doorway: *Naalu Pennungal* and *Oru Pennum Randaanum*

1 Adoor Gopalakrishnan in conversation with the author, April 2013.

7. Making the Imaginary Real: *Anantaram*, *Mathilukal* and *Nizhalkkuthu*

1 C. S.Venkiteswaran. "A Door to Adoor." In *A Door to Adoor*, edited by Lalit Mohan Joshi and C. S. Venkiteswaran. London: South Asian Cinema Foundation, 2006: 85.
2 Adoor Gopalakrishnan "The Director on the Film." In *Monologue*, edited by Shampa Banerjee. Calcutta: Seagull Press, 1991: 7.
3 Adoor Gopalakrishnan in conversation with the author, October 2009.
4 During British rule, India's handloom textile industry was seriously threatened by the import of cloth made in the mills of Lancashire and India. Gandhi asked for the

boycott of such mill-made cloth in favor of hand-woven cloth spun by using the *charka* or weaver's wheel. The *charka* quickly became a national symbol of self-sufficiency and the fight against exploitation.

8. The Dream of Emancipation: *Kathapurushan* and the Triumph of the Individual

1 Pradeep Dharmapalan. "An Outsider Looking In." *Gulf News Tabloid*, January 16, 1997: 5.
2 Suranjan Ganguly. "Mapping Interiors: An Interview with Adoor Gopalakrishnan." *Asian Cinema* 9, no. 1 (1997): 15.
3 Ibid.
4 Ibid.

BIBLIOGRAPHY

Armand, Martine. "Notes on Adoor Gopalakrishnan's Cinema." *Festival de Films de Fribourg* brochure (1997): 114–28.
Bhaskaran, Gautaman. *Adoor Gopalakrishnan: A Life in Cinema*. New Delhi: Penguin India, 2010.
Chatterjee, Saibal. "Master's Vision." *Outlook*, April 2, 1997.
Da Cunha, Uma. "*Kodiyettam*." In *Film India: The New Generation, 1960–1980*, edited by Uma da Cunha, 87. New Delhi: Directorate of Film Festivals, 1981.
Datta, Aloknanda, and Soma Roy. "Adoor Gopalakrishnan in Conversation." *Splice* 2 (1986): 23–30.
Datta, Ella. "Authority and the Individual." *Telegraph*, Calcutta, September 10, 2000.
Datta, Sangeeta. *Shyam Benegal*. London: British Film Institute, 2008.
Dharmapalan, Pradeep. "An Outsider Looking In." *Gulf News Tabloid*, January 16, 1997.
Donmez-Colin, Gonul. "Aesthetics of Politics: Adoor Gopalakrishnan." *Deep Focus* 8, nos. 1–2 (1998): 91–96.
Gopalakrishnan, Adoor. "Adoor on Adoor Films." In *Adoor Gopalakrishnan: Twenty Five Years of Filmmaking*, edited by S. B. Jayaram, 32–44. Trivandrum: Chalachithra, 1996.
———. "The Director about the Film." In *Face to Face*, edited by Shampa Banerjee, n.p. Calcutta: Seagull Press, 1985.
———. "The Director on the Film." In *Monologue*, edited by Shampa Banerjee, 7. Calcutta: Seagull Press, 1991.
———. "Satyajit Ray." In *Satyajit Ray at 70*, edited by Nemai Ghosh and Alok Nandi, 95–96. Hyderabad: Orient Longman, 1992.
Ganguly, Suranjan. "Mapping Interiors: An Interview with Adoor Gopalakrishnan." *Asian Cinema* 9, no. 1 (1997): 1–17.
Halter, Ed. "Final Destination: The God of Small Things." *Village Voice*, April 30–May 6, 2003. Accessed January 6, 2012. http://www.villagevoice.com/film/0318,halter43698,20.html
Hood, John W. *The Essential Mystery*. Hyderabad: Orient Longman, 2000.
Joshi, Lalit Mohan, and C. S. Venkiteswaran, eds. *A Door to Adoor*. London: South Asian Cinema Foundation, 2006.
———. "*Nizhalkkuthu*—The Epic Conflict." In *A Door to Adoor*, edited by Lalit Mohan Joshi and C. S. Venkiteswaran, 112–16. London: South Asian Cinema Foundation, 2006.
Krishnakumar, R. "Cinema with a Purpose." *Frontline*, August 9–22, 1997. Accessed January 7, 2013. http://www.the-hindu.com/fline/fl1416/14161560.htm
Mohamed, Khalid. "The Unseen Woman." *Times of India*, March 4, 1990.
Nair, P. K. "Some Memorable Moments in Adoor's Films." In *A Door to Adoor*, edited by Lalit Mohan Joshi and C. S. Venkiteswaran, 120–25. London: South Asian Cinema Foundation, 2006.

Nossiter, T. J. *Communism in Kerala*. Berkeley and Los Angeles: University of California Press, 1982.

Rajadhyaksha, Ashish. "Adoor Gopalakrishnan." In *Encyclopaedia of Indian Cinema*, edited by Ashish Rajadhyaksha and Paul Willemen, 97. London: British Film Institute, 1994.

———. "Elippathayam—Film Plot and Review." Accessed March 24, 2013. http://www.filmreference.com/Films-Dr-Ex/Elippathayam.html

Rao, Maithili. "Adoor Gopalakrishnan—The Apolitical Humanist Projects the Sky on a Dew Drop." In *A Door to Adoor*, edited by Lalit Mohan Joshi and C. S. Venkiteswaran, 33–44. London: South Asian Cinema Foundation, 2006.

Santosh, K. "Decades of Struggle and Surprise." *Hindu*, November 28, 1997. Accessed January 7, 2013. http://www.webpage.com/hindu/daily/971128/09

Singh, Bikram. "Anybody Who Says It Is an Anti-Marxist Film Has Absolutely Not Understood It." *Sunday Observer*, December 2, 1984.

Spinelli, Italo. "Interview with Adoor Gopalakrishnan." *Indian Summer*, Locarno Film Festival brochure, 2002. Accessed January 10, 2010. http://www.kagw.com/adoor/italo_spiineeli_interview.htm

Srinivasan, Rajeev. "The Movie Interview." *Rediff on the Net*, July 31, 1997. Accessed February 7, 2011. http://www.redifindia.com/entertai/jul31adoor.htm

Tharayil, Muraleedharan. "*Elippathayam: Rat Trap.*" In *Cinema of India*, edited by Lalitha Gopalan, 191–199. London and New York: Wallflower Press, 2010.

Thoraval, Yves. *Cinemas of India*. New Delhi: Macmillan India, 2000.

Vausudev, Aruna. "Adoor Gopalakrishnan: Beyond the Wall." *Cinemaya* 22 (1994): 14–23.

Venkiteswaran, C. S. "A Door to Adoor." In *A Door to Adoor*, edited by Lalit Mohan Joshi and C. S. Venkiteswaran, 52–111. London: South Asian Cinema Foundation, 2006.

———. "Contemporary Malayalam Cinema." 2007. Accessed March 13, 2013. http://www.bfi.org.uk/features/imagineasia/guide/contemporary/malayalam.html

———. "*Swayamvaram*—Classic Prophecies." In *A Door to Adoor*, edited by Lalit Mohan Joshi and C. S. Venkiteswaran, 27–32. London: South Asian Cinema Foundation, 2006.

Walsh, Bryan. "Knee Deep in the New Wave." *Time*, April 28, 2003. Accessed January 7, 2013. http://www.time.com/time/printout/0,8816,447254,00.html

Warrier, Shobha. "You Want the Audience to Come and Watch Your Film on Your Terms, Not Theirs." *Sunday Observer*, July 21–27, 1996.

ABOUT THE AUTHOR

Suranjan Ganguly is from Calcutta, India. He studied at St. Xavier's College and Jadavpur University before coming to the United States. He received his doctorate degree from Purdue University, Indiana, and teaches a wide range of courses in European and Asian cinema at the University of Colorado at Boulder. Ganguly is the author of *Satyajit Ray: In Search of the Modern* (2000), and his work has appeared in *Sight and Sound,* the *East-West Film Journal, Asian Cinema, South Asian Cinema,* the *Journal of Commonwealth Literature, Film Criticism,* the *Journal of South Asian Literature* and *Film Culture.* He is currently editing the interviews of Stan Brakhage for the University Press of Mississippi.

INDEX

Abraham, John 11–12
alcoholism 5, 45
Anantaram 4, 6, 14, 111, 112–3, 125, 131, 139
Ankur 11
Aravindan, Govindan 11–12
ayurvedic 147–8

Basheer, Vaikom Muhammad 9, 121
Benegal, Shyam 11–12
Bhagavatham 24
bhakti 9
Bhaskara Patelarum Ente Jeevithavum 45
Bildungsroman 141
Bollywood 11–13

charka 134, 160
Chinnu Amma 99–101
Chitralekha Film Cooperative 11
Chitralekha Film Society 11
Christian 48, 54, 59, 60
communism 7, 8, 16, 30, 148
Communist Party 7, 15, 63, 151
Communist Party of India (CPI) 7, 15
Communist Party of India Marxist (CPI-M) 7, 15
consumption 14, 63, 65

Datta, Sangeeta 12
dislocation 2, 9, 31, 65, 80, 153
displaced 3, 48, 111
displacement 2, 8, 13, 32, 43, 65, 84, 104, 109
doorway 14, 55–6, 69, 95–6, 99, 101–3, 105–7, 109, 143

Elippathayam 4, 6, 8, 13–14, 31–44, 45, 51, 58, 80
emancipation 4–5, 13–14, 30, 32, 44, 60, 63, 77, 80, 96–7, 109, 112, 134, 139, 141, 153, 154
Emergency 142, 152

enslavement 50, 53–4, 56, 61, 83
eviction 2, 48, 51, 84
ex-feudal 4, 8

feudal 2, 7–8, 33, 39, 40–1, 43, 46–7, 60, 132, 141–4, 146, 148–53
feudalism 7, 31, 39, 46, 48, 63, 133, 141, 149
Film and Television Institute of India 9

Gandhi, Indira 142, 152
Gandhi, M. K. 7, 121, 133–4, 139, 142, 146, 148–9, 151
Ghatak, Ritwik 9, 10
gluttony 5, 64, 65, 98
Gopalakrishnan, Adoor 1–14
guilt 2, 4, 13, 23, 28, 41, 43, 46, 48, 54–5, 57–9, 60, 70–2, 80, 86, 88–9, 91–2, 94, 101, 104, 108–9, 115, 117–9, 132–4, 149

Hard Consonants, The 141, 152
home 2, 9, 13, 14, 23, 31, 39, 48, 51, 76–7, 80–1, 83–4, 98–9, 104, 109, 120, 141, 143–6
homelessness 31, 48, 96
homoeroticism 51
humanism 10, 146, 153–4

identity crisis 8
imaginary 2, 4, 7, 14–17, 21, 27, 52, 96, 111–2, 116–7, 120–2, 124, 129, 131–2, 137, 139
Indian New Wave 9, 11–13, 79
India's independence 7–8, 12, 46, 103, 131, 148, 153–4
interiority 3, 6, 111

Kallante Makan 105–6
Kanyaka 97–9
Karnataka 12, 45, 48
Kathakali 6, 9, 77

Kathapurushan 4, 8, 13, 14, 31, 141–54
Kerala 2–5, 7–8, 11–13, 15–17, 31–2, 48, 50, 63, 65–6, 79–80, 95–6, 103, 132–3, 141–2, 151–3
Kodiyettam 3, 5–6, 8, 14, 63–77, 79, 80, 98
Kutiyattam 6–7

Land Reforms Bill 7, 142, 146
Left Front Alliance 152
Lenin 18–19, 22–4
liminality 2, 3, 13, 96

machismo 63, 75
Mahabharata 138
Malayalam cinema 9, 11
Malayalam language 1, 11, 132
Malayalam literary renaissance 9
Malayalam literature 9, 121
Mani, Kaul 9–10
marriage 65–6, 75, 77, 79–80, 86–7, 96–9, 102, 107, 118
masculinity 5, 14, 63
Mathilukal 4, 6, 14, 111–2, 121–31, 139
matrilineal 7, 9, 32, 66, 95, 148–9
modernity 2, 8–9, 12–13, 31, 63, 80, 94, 133, 141, 143, 147–8, 153
motherhood 99–100, 104
Mukhamukham 3–4, 6–8, 14, 15–30, 32, 94, 111–3, 121, 124–5, 141–2, 154

Naalu Pennungal 9, 14, 95–105
Nairs 9, 32
nalukettu 32–3, 38, 40
National Film Development Corporation of India 11
nationalism 7, 9
Naxalites 151
Nehru, Jawaharlal 7, 8, 63, 80
Nitya Kanyaka 101–5
Nizhalkkuthu 4, 13–14, 111–2, 131–6, 139, 153
nizhalkkuthu 138
Niyamvum Neethiyum 96

Oru Koottukaran 106–7
Oru Niyamalanghanathinte Katha 96–7
Oru Pennum Randaanum 9, 14, 95–6, 105–9
Other 3, 45, 74, 96, 113, 122, 132, 135–6, 139, 144
otherness 2, 3, 7, 13, 16, 31, 36, 48, 63, 79, 84, 95, 104, 109, 111–2, 114, 127, 132, 134–9, 142

outsider 3, 13, 15, 19, 31, 36, 40–1, 45, 50–1, 58–9, 63, 80, 84, 104, 111, 113, 115–6, 121, 132, 139, 145, 150, 152

Pankiyamma 106–9
Parallel Cinema 12–13
Pather Panchali 10
Pillai, Thakazi Sivasankara 9, 96
poomukham 33, 42
post-feudal 5, 14, 31–2, 45, 48
Progressive Writers 9
provider 38, 65, 68–72, 76–7, 89, 95, 106
pudava 77

Quit India movement 121
quotidian 5, 37, 64, 74, 129

Rajadhyaksha, Ashish 8, 10
Rama 89, 149
Ramayana 89, 90
Ravana 89, 90
Ray, Satyajit 1, 10
realism 2–3, 5–6, 7, 9–10, 17–18, 19, 24, 29, 79, 81–2, 117, 119, 120, 121–4, 128, 138, 139
redemption 2, 10, 13, 15, 43, 54–5, 59–60
regional cinemas 12–3
resistance 42–3, 51, 56, 58

Sen, Mrinal 10
servile 34, 39, 49, 50, 53, 58, 59
servility 2, 34, 46, 48, 50–1, 52–3, 56, 59–60
Shahani, Kumar 9
Sita 89
subjectivity 2, 113
swayamvara 89, 90
Swayamvaram 6, 8, 11, 14, 79–94, 96

tarawad 32
thali 87
transcendence 2, 5, 14, 45, 60, 96, 112, 122–3, 129, 131, 154
Travancore 7, 96, 131, 133–4

Vidheyan 4–5, 8, 14, 31, 45–61, 80, 153

yajamanan 144, 146, 150, 153
yajamanare 46, 49, 52–3, 57, 59

Zacharia, Paul 45

www.ingramcontent.com/pod-product-compliance
Lightning Source LLC
Chambersburg PA
CBHW021830300426
44114CB00009BA/397